PUT DOWN YOUR SWORD

Put Down Your Sword

ANSWERING THE GOSPEL CALL
TO CREATIVE NONVIOLENCE

John Dear

William B. Eerdmans Publishing Company

Grand Rapids, Michigan / Cambridge, U.K.

Published 2008 by
Wm. B. Eerdmans Publishing Co.
2140 Oak Industrial Drive N.E., Grand Rapids, Michigan 49505 /
P.O. Box 163, Cambridge CB3 9PU U.K.

Printed in the United States of America

13 12 11 10 09 08   7 6 5 4 3 2 1

Library of Congress Cataloging-in-Publication Data

Dear, John, 1959-
Put down your sword: answering the Gospel call to creative nonviolence / John Dear.
p.   cm.
Includes bibliographical references and index.
ISBN 978-0-8028-6357-7 (pbk.: alk. paper)
1. Nonviolence — Religious aspects — Catholic Church.
2. Peace — Religious aspects — Catholic Church.
3. Catholic Church — Doctrines.   I. Title.

BX1795.N66D45   2008
241'.697 — dc22

2008010811

www.eerdmans.com

For Joan Baez

Contents

Introduction

Each day we hear some new tale of horror and woe — fifty killed in a Baghdad market, thirty students shot dead at a Virginia university, hundreds killed in a hurricane, rising sea levels, U.S.-funded Israeli attacks on Palestinians, widespread HIV/AIDS epidemics in Africa, thousands dying each year crossing the Mexican border, massive funding for a new generation of nuclear weapons, yet further cutbacks for schools, jobs, health care, housing — and so forth. The bad news is so prevalent, so heralded, so celebrated that it all but blocks out any good news. Indeed, some of us forget that there is such a thing as good news.

As I study the lives of the saints and the peacemakers, I discover that they turned a deaf ear to the bad news, that they listened close to the good news, and that they even worked to generate more good news. They lived in hope because they did hopeful things. Most of all, they looked to the example and teachings of Jesus and tried to live accordingly, to apply those teachings to the world. As they did, they became good news for others. Just as Jesus gave people hope, they gave people hope.

Jesus was the greatest practitioner of nonviolence in the history of the world. In our times of total violence, global warming, and perpetual war, he offers good news at every level — personally, communally, socially, economically, spiritually, and politically. He points to a way out, a way forward, a way toward a new world of peace.

For over twenty-five years now, I have experimented with his teachings of Gospel nonviolence, his good news of peace. My work for peace and justice has taken me across the country and around the world. These days, when I'm not on the road, preaching the good news of peace, I live alone on a mesa in the high desert of New Mexico and work with a campaign to disarm Los Alamos, the birthplace of the bomb. My friends and I want to be part of the good news, to hear the good news, to generate good news in a bad time.

This little book offers some musings, reflections, lessons, and observations from my recent journeys and experiments with Gospel nonviolence. In the first section I share my convictions and insights about the nonviolence of Jesus, the Beatitudes, the nature of God, and the mystery of the resurrection. In the second section I relate stories from our protests against the Los Alamos Nuclear Weapons Laboratories, the School of the Americas, and the U.S. war on Iraq. The third section features the journals I kept on missions to Gandhi's India and war-torn Colombia. In the fourth section I reflect on the peacemakers who inspire me most these days — from legendary figures such as Dr. Martin Luther King, Thich Nhat Hanh, and César Chávez, to priests like Henri Nouwen and Bill O'Donnell, to poets like Joan Baez and Denise Levertov, to resisters like Sophie Scholl and Franz Jägerstätter. In the final section I offer reflections on care for the earth, the teachings of Thomas Merton, and the vision of a new world without war, poverty, violence, or nuclear weapons.

I offer these pages as a word of hope to encourage you to take another step on your journey of Gospel nonviolence, despite the horrors of our violent world and the hopelessness that would keep us down. I believe we are intended to live in peace — with ourselves, one another, all humanity, all creation, and the God of peace — and that such a life, individually and globally, is possible. We cannot wait to receive it as a gift from the culture of war. We need to live it now as a sign of our faith in the God of peace, as a clue to our entrance into God's reign of peace, as a gift to one another, as a way into hope for ourselves and the whole human race.

I pray that these reflections inspire you on your journey to peace and embolden you to pursue the coming of a new world without war, poverty, violence, or nuclear weapons, a new world of nonviolence, with even greater hope, that you too might hear the good news and take heart once more.

JOHN DEAR

I will listen for the word of God; surely the LORD will proclaim peace
To his people, to the faithful, to those who trust in him.
Near indeed is salvation for the loyal; prosperity will fill our land.

Love and truth will meet; justice and peace will kiss;
Truth will spring from the earth; justice will look down from heaven.
The LORD will surely grant abundance; our land will yield its increase.
Prosperity will march before the Lord, and good fortune will follow behind.

PSALM 85:9-14 (NAB)

PART I

The Commandments of Gospel Nonviolence

Jesus lived and died in vain if he did not teach us to regulate the whole of life by the eternal law of love.

MAHATMA GANDHI

The only message I have to the world is: we are not allowed to kill innocent people. We are not allowed to be complicit in murder. We are not allowed to be silent while preparations for mass murder proceed in our name with our money, secretly. . . . Our plight is very primitive from a Christian point of view. We are back where we started. Thou shalt not kill. We are not allowed to kill. Everything today comes down to that — everything.

DANIEL BERRIGAN

CHAPTER 1

The Last Words of Jesus

A few years ago I met one of the key leaders of the Christian evangelical movement in the United States. He had served for decades as Billy Graham's assistant and organizer of the National Prayer breakfast. He felt passionately about the Gospel of Jesus, had spent time with Mother Teresa and made retreats at the Abbey of Gethsemani. I was invited to spend a morning with him sharing and praying together.

What does one say to such a prestigious Christian? We shook hands, and I asked him point-blank, "As the soldiers approached Jesus in the Garden of Gethsemani, what were his last words? In other words, what were the last words to the church before he was killed?"

My new friend looked at me. He didn't know.

"Put down the sword." Jesus spent his life teaching and practicing creative nonviolence, I explained. He commanded us to love our enemies and become blessed peacemakers. He forbade violence, killing, and wars, once and for all times. We are not allowed to kill, no matter how noble the cause. Period.

As the soldiers laid hold of Jesus, I reflected, one of his disciples drew his sword and struck — a follower of Jesus employing the soldier's tactics. A disciple unnamed, according to the Gospels of Matthew, Mark, and Luke, but John's Gospel names the man. The sword-wielding disciple was none other than Peter himself. Hardly a hero. We learn later that, as Jesus' trial gets underway, Peter denies he knows Jesus at all. Perhaps Peter resorted to violence not to protect Jesus but to save his own sweet skin.

As I travel the nation and the world, speaking about Gospel nonviolence to large audiences and small retreat gatherings, many people respond to me like this: "Well, John, this peace stuff is all well and good, and nonviolence is a beautiful ideal, and Jesus certainly was a nice guy. But sometimes you just have to kill someone. Sometimes war is justified. The churches were right long ago. Throw out the Sermon on the Mount, and when certain conditions are met, any violence is justified violence. We really do have to kill Hitler, or Noriega, or Saddam, or Osama (or whomever we're told from time to time we're supposed to kill)."

I then proceed to explain that if ever there was a moment when the just-war theory might apply, when violence would be divinely sanctioned and justified, it's in that garden scene moments before Jesus is arrested and hauled off to his execution. This one moment stands as the ultimate point in history in which violence could have been applied. Peter is right. He's thinking that his primary duty as a disciple is to protect this guy, "the holy innocent one." He is correct: take out the sword and start killing people to make sure that Jesus is not arrested or taken away.

Just at that precise moment, as Peter raises the sword to kill in order to protect Jesus, the commandment comes down: "Put down the sword."

I think this is also the moment when the disciples finally understand Jesus and his teachings. They suddenly realize that he is deadly serious about peace, love, and nonviolence. He's so committed to nonviolence that he's not even going to defend himself with violence. I imagine them agape as this revelation unfolds before them. What do they do? They immediately run off, every man for himself.

And Jesus? He's arrested, jailed, mocked, tried, tortured, and executed, and he never once strikes back with retaliatory violence, never once explodes with anger, never once condemns anyone. He's unarmed, nonviolent, vulnerable, alone, and prayerful. As he dies, he shows compassion on his murderers and forgives them. As Gandhi noted, Jesus practiced the most perfect nonviolence in history. I regard Jesus as the incarnation of nonviolence, the embodiment of the God of love and peace. His nonviolence is the key to understanding Christian discipleship today. He teaches us everything — how to live, how to love, how to pray, how to suffer, how to die — everything but how to kill.

We have spent the last seventeen hundred years denying Jesus' final command. We have justified warfare, led crusades, and stamped every bombing raid and nuclear weapon with our blessing. Over and over again, we betray him, deny him, and disobey him as we support the world's wars.

But the commandment remains: "Put down the sword." I think one day the church will realize that the just-war theory has no place in the Gospel of Jesus. They'll realize it goes against everything for which Jesus stood and lived and died. On that day, the theory will fall into disrepute. As the late Bishop Dozier said, it will be put away in the same drawer as the "flat earth theory." I think that most churchgoers secretly know that Jesus was nonviolent and taught nonviolence, that he would never justify violence, war, or nuclear weapons. If we are so adamant in our disobedience to Jesus in this area, why don't we have other theories of justified violence — "the just adultery theory," "the just abortion theory," "the just death-penalty theory," "the just global-warming theory," "the just racism theory," "the just sexism theory"? That would be absurd.

One day the church will wake up, reject violence and warfare once and for all, and teach only Gospel nonviolence. Christians everywhere will quit the military and refuse to join. They'll obstruct warfare and beat swords into plowshares. They'll obey Jesus and spread the good news of nonviolence with the same passion as Mahatma Gandhi, Dorothy Day, and Martin Luther King Jr.

After I had said my piece, my new friend sat silent for a moment. A look of thoughtfulness settled over his face, and he said, "That is a very important observation." I pressed him further. How seriously do we want to take the commandments of Jesus? How far do we go on the journey of nonviolence in our own lives? What does the cross of nonviolent, suffering love mean in a world of total violence and war? We can pray, go to church, read about Jesus, write about him, preach about him, and organize influential gatherings about him. But I think Jesus wants foremost for us to obey him. He wants us to return to the roots of the early church and put down our swords, renounce violent self-defense, tear up the just-war theory, abolish our weapons, end our wars, resist injustice, feed the hungry, house the homeless, reconcile with all people, and practice universal, nonviolent love.

The unarmed Christ wants his community, the church, to be a community of creative, loving nonviolence. The greatest challenge before us at this terrible moment in history is finally to take Jesus at his word — to put down the sword and become a church of nonviolence, a people of nonviolence.

CHAPTER 2

The Beatitudes of Peace

Open your Bible to Matthew 5 and you will never be the same. Gandhi and King called those passages the grandest manifesto of nonviolence ever written — beginning with the storied Beatitudes. Grand for a number of obvious reasons — for their poignancy and conciseness, for their sheer poetics, for their morality and practicality. But grand, too, for a subtle reason — for the furtive critique that lies behind them. Namely, every culture of war, such as Jesus lived and died in, fuels itself by an antithetical set of maxims. One might name them "the anti-Beatitudes."

They are easily reconstructed because, alas, they're all too familiar. We've been tutored in them all our lives; they hang in the air, live in our very bones. This false spirituality of violence, injustice, and war is what Jesus spoke out against. He countered every anti-Beatitude.

"Blessed are the rich; the reign of this world is ours."
Empirically the rich rule the world, and the rest suffer and die, often in misery. But Jesus counters with the real truth. Blessed are the poor in spirit, those who have nothing — no power, no prestige, no possessions, no success. They receive the first and greatest blessing: entrance into God's reign. The rich lay claim to all things except that. Thus Jesus calls us to live in friendship with the poor, to let go of power and domination, to embrace our own powerlessness. Which is to say, if we share our lives with the poor and practice downward mobility, they will share with us the reign of God.

The Pentagon's chief tenet: "Blessed are those who make others mourn."
Those who kill, who support war, who pay taxes for killing, who build

nuclear weapons, who execute people — blessed are they, the Pentagon insists. More, blessed are you if you never mourn. But Jesus sets this anti-Beatitude right. He says, Blessed are the billions who mourn their loved ones lost to starvation, injustice, relievable disease, and war — from Hiroshima and Vietnam to El Salvador and Iraq. God's consolation will flow to them. As for us, mourning leads to peacemaking. As we mourn with those who mourn, we receive God's consolation. Otherwise, no comfort will be ours.

The motto of every warlike culture: "Blessed are the violent and the invincible, the proud and the powerful, the domineering and the oppressive."

But Jesus says the meek are blessed — the gentle, the humble, the nonviolent. The violent inherit nothing but blood and destruction. The meek — they inherit the earth. Pursuing nonviolence wins the blessing of creation itself. As St. Francis discovered, creation and nonviolence are inextricably linked.

"Blessed are those who hunger and thirst for injustice."

This is the siren song of the System. The System sustains itself by all manner of injustice and lawlessness and greed. But Jesus offers a contrary word. Desire for unjust gain shall forever thwart fulfillment. The unjust will never be satisfied. But those who are passionate for justice will find satisfaction, true meaning. They'll take part in God's very purpose: the transformation of disarmament and global peace.

"Blessed are those who show no mercy."

So the culture summons us. No mercy to the poor, to women and children, the elderly and the homeless, victims, outcasts, enemies, refugees, the hungry, the undocumented, the unborn, those on death row, those who are gay and lesbian, those who are different, those we don't like. But the culture keeps the spiritual consequence close to its vest: The merciless will be shown no mercy. On the other hand, says Jesus, God's mercy comes to the merciful.

"Blessed are the impure of heart."

The warlike culture tells us that it does not matter if we are filled with darkness and confusion and violence. But such darkness, says Jesus, shades our view of God. It obscures our recognition of Christ in the poor, in the enemy, in one another.

Rather, "Blessed are the pure in heart" — those with disarmed hearts, nonviolent hearts, hearts of universal love. To attain such wholehearted love, we must practice contemplative prayer, turn our violence over to God, and receive in return God's gift of peace. Thus illumined by the light of God, we'll see God in the struggle for justice, in the bread and the cup, in creation, in the poor, in the enemy. The pure in heart will see God. The beatific vision will begin here and now.

"Blessed are the warmakers."

Thus say the president, the Pentagon and its chaplains. No, says Jesus. "Blessed are the peacemakers" — those who help end war and the conditions for war, who create peace. They are sons and daughters of the living God. Peace is God's purpose for humanity. God is a God of peace. Since we are God's children, we make peace too.

The warlike culture tries to name us its patriots, warriors, "good" Americans. It wants to tell us who we are. But Jesus tells us the truth: we are the beloved sons and daughters of the God of peace. That means, like Jesus, we act according to the God of peace, practice nonviolence, resist war, demand that the troops come home from Iraq, and try to live and breathe the Holy Spirit of peace.

"Blessed are those who never stand up for justice, who do not rock the boat."

The silent, the indifferent, the comfortable, those who keep their distance. Blessed are you — you've made it! You'll ruffle no feathers and invite no trouble — but neither will you possess the reign of God.

The reign of God belongs to those "persecuted for the sake of justice." In a world where war and nuclear weapons run wild, peacemakers get no thanks, no honors. They're harassed, threatened, put under surveillance, arrested, jailed, even killed. But Jesus says, This is your opportunity to practice nonviolence, to meet hatred with love — just like the prophets and the saints.

8

So Jesus declares, "Blessed are you when people insult you and persecute you and utter every kind of evil against you falsely because of me. Rejoice and be glad, for your reward will be great in heaven." Do we draw
heat for our work against poverty, the death penalty, nuclear weapons, the
war on Iraq? Take heart — rejoice and be glad. We're on the right path. We
are joining the ranks of Mahatma Gandhi, Martin Luther King, Dorothy
Day, Archbishop Romero, Ita Ford, and Dorothy Stang.

Recently I learned that some scholars are rethinking the original
Greek translation of the Beatitudes. The passive "Blessed are . . ." is not
accurate, they say. Better the more active phrase: "Walk on! Walk forth!"
If true, it sounds a different tone, a tone of doggedness, support, encouragement. God cheers us on, that we might go the distance in pursuit of
justice and peace. The "active" Beatitudes might read something like
this:

Walk forth, you poor in spirit, you humble and powerless. Keep going.
   Don't be discouraged by your poverty. The reign of God is yours.
Walk forth, you who mourn the victims of war and hunger. Keep going.
   You will be consoled.
Walk forth, you meek and gentle and nonviolent. Inherit the earth and
   enjoy the blessing of creation.
Walk forth, you who hunger and thirst for justice. Don't give up. You
   will be satisfied. "Justice will roll down like waters, and righteous-
   ness like a mighty stream."
Walk forth, you merciful. Keep showing mercy in a merciless world.
   Forgive everyone. Be compassionate to everyone. Show mercy to everyone. Mercy will be yours.
Walk forth, you pure in heart. Keep going. Be filled with the light of
   peace and see Christ in the poor, in the enemy, in one another.
Walk forth, you who make peace. Keep going. Speak against war. Organize peace vigils. Write Congress, demand that the troops come
   home, work for nuclear disarmament. Become who you are, the
   sons and daughters of the God of peace.
Walk forth, you who are persecuted for justice. Keep going. Don't give
   up. You stand on the shoulders of other great justice-seekers before
   you. Your reward will be great.

Here are the Beatitudes of Peace, uttered contrary to the anti-Beatitudes of war that pulse through the veins of our culture. If we follow these guideposts, hear this encouragement, we learn, the Gospel teaches, that the God of peace is alive and at work among us — giving us God's reign, God's consolation, God's creation, God's satisfaction, God's mercy, God's face, God's calling us her daughters and sons, and God's best reward. In other words, take heart. God is leading us into the fullness of life. All we have to do is walk the narrow path of nonviolence, live the life of peace, and enjoy the blessings.

CHAPTER 3

Our Image of God

Recently my Jesuit brother Daniel Berrigan and I spent an evening with Franciscan priest and teacher Richard Rohr at the Catholic Worker house in Albuquerque. A blizzard swirled outside, and the conversation inside swirled nearly as briskly. Dan and I had spent the day touring Los Alamos, birthplace of the atomic bomb. We came away shocked by business as usual, an entire culture, a worldview, a way of being, built around the bomb.

A culture of peace, on the other hand, rises from the Catholic Worker, and the conversation soon turned to the nonviolent Jesus and the God of peace. Richard said he now thinks the church's ancient teaching of a theology of sacrifice has helped bring about our culture of violence. For eons we've been told that God, out of some vague need, variously explained over the centuries, required Jesus to be killed in order to save us. The time has arrived, Richard said, for a new theology of nonviolent atonement, a theology that upholds the nonviolence of God and Jesus.

Richard has thought this through. He cites St. Paul's letters to the Philippians and Colossians, both of which poetically and accurately characterize Jesus as "the image of the invisible God." If the portrait rings true, then all we've believed about divine violence proves false.

Jesus reveals a God of perfect nonviolent love. Throughout his life, death, and resurrection, he manifested perfect love, compassion, and nonviolence. "Nothing changed on Calvary," Richard said. Jesus was nonviolent before, during, and after. After his death, he punished no one, condemned no one, sought revenge against no one. His life rises to the ultimate revelation of divine nonviolence.

I heartily agree with Richard Rohr. The hallmark of the Gospel message is the summons to love God, neighbor — and even our enemies. Surprisingly, Jesus commands us to love our enemies not because it is the right, the moral, or the practical thing to do. He commands it because God loves enemies. God lavishes love widely, promiscuously, universally.

Jesus says, do likewise "that you may be children of your heavenly God, for God makes the sun rise on the bad and the good, and causes rain to fall on the just and the unjust. . . . So be perfect, just as your heavenly God is perfect" (Matt. 5:45-48). Here is nonviolence showered upon every human being. And Christians are called to follow suit.

The Gospel portrays Jesus' nonviolence as the ultimate scandal. Even the disciples recoil. The scandal and recoiling go on. Today Christians support the war on Iraq, cheer the execution of the condemned, build nuclear weapons at Los Alamos. One concludes that the notion of a nonviolent God is just too much to bear. We rarely take a moment to ponder it. And to some degree we, all of us, pursue a false image of God. One that wishes to banish us to hell, that prefers us to suffer, that blesses injustice and war — a god, so to speak, made in our own violent image. And thus we walk through life undisturbed by revenge, punishment, executions, and war. At Los Alamos, we see it plain: We worship the false god of war.

But the Gospel holds up Jesus' nonviolence in an honorific light. If he is indeed the image of the invisible God, then God is nonviolent because Jesus was meticulously so. This is, in my view, the opening to mystery and divinity. Saint Ignatius seems to have had similar notions. Jesuit spirituality long ago directed the seeker to reflect on his or her image of God. Ignatius knew it was critical to our lives, our spirituality, our faith, our future. Whom do we worship? What is our image of God? Is our God violent or nonviolent?

Gandhi, too, drew attention to one's image of God and shed a measure of light on the social and political implications of that. Imagine God as violent, he suggested, and worship devolves into the countenancing of scapegoating and bloodletting, by our hand or in our name. Revenge and war proceed apace — and us scarcely batting an eye. In such a time as this, we risk dooming ourselves to global annihilation.

But imagine God as nonviolent, and worship takes on the fragrance of peace. We enter a deep mystery and bow our heads in awe and wonder and finally, ever so gradually, in imitation of the God of love, evolve into people of nonviolence and peace.

The culture of war discounts all this. Its grumbling takes a form something like this: "Such talk is tantamount to heresy. Let go of the vengeful image of God, and what becomes of boundaries? What becomes of order? Worse, such talk amounts to flagrant defiance, stubborn nonconformity, perhaps an act of resistance punishable by law!" The culture of war always tries to instruct us on the nature of God, the definition of sin and morality, the way to be Christian, even human. It knows only "sacred" violence and a god of thunderbolts and fury. And mushroom clouds.

Thus the task at hand: to envision the God of peace. For our souls and for the world. The more we envision and grasp the image of the God of peace, the more we'll fathom Jesus' teachings, comprehend how to be human, become a peacemaking church of all-inclusive love, and come upon a way or two to help disarm a world armed to the teeth.

Theology, say the professors, is "God talk" — simply put, talking about God. Ignatius and Gandhi engaged in it. Richard, Daniel, and I, along with our Catholic Worker friends, engaged in it. And I hope we can all keep at that spiritual conversation, sharing our reflections on Jesus and the God of peace, so that we grow in faith and get drawn more and more into the mystery of divine nonviolence.

CHAPTER 4

The Politics of the Sacred Heart

Call me old-fashioned, but I love everything about the old Catholic image of the Sacred Heart of Jesus, where he points to his heart aflame with light and love. In recent years, however, I've begun to wonder: What are the social, economic, and political implications of the Sacred Heart of Jesus? That question, I believe, can lead us to a whole new world of love, compassion, forgiveness, nonviolence, and justice, to our own disarmed, sacred hearts.

I know some like this image because it projects a safe, nonthreatening God. It demonstrates the enormity of God's love for humanity and calls us to disarm our own hearts, that we too might be gentle, nonviolent, compassionate, and perpetually loving. I figure most people tend to ignore that this gentle Jesus also denounced injustice, turned over the tables in the Temple, and was arrested, jailed, tortured, and executed.

But there's more to the story. On December 29, 1673, when Jesus appeared to St. Margaret Mary Alacoque in Paray-le-Monial, France, he said, "My divine heart is so impassioned with love for humanity, it cannot contain the flames of its burning charity inside. It must spread them through you and show itself to humanity so that they may be enriched by the previous treasures that I share with you, treasures which have all the sanctifying and saving graces needed to draw them back from the abyss of destruction."

The abyss of destruction? Poor Margaret Mary probably didn't have a clue about what Jesus meant, but we sure do. Today we stand at the brink of unprecedented global destruction, global warming, and global violence. This violence pushes us personally and internationally ever closer to the abyss of destruction, but the grace of the Sacred Heart — with all its burning social, economic, and political implications — has the power to convert us into people of Gospel nonviolence, to pull us back from the brink and create a new world of peace with justice.

The Sacred Heart of Jesus is our way out of the madness of war, violence, and injustice. But who thinks of the "abyss of destruction" in light of the Sacred Heart of Jesus? If we were to adopt the image of the Sacred Heart of Jesus as our image of a nonviolent, peacemaking God, and live not just individually but communally, nationally, and globally according to that nonviolent, radiant love, the world would be disarmed.

The image of the Sacred Heart invites us to practice universal love, eternal forgiveness, infinite compassion, active nonviolence, and perfect peace. That means, among other things, that we can no longer support killing, injustice, war, or any other kind of violence. It means further that we must live out a new ethic and create new nonviolent structures that institutionalize nonviolent love, dignity, and peace for every human being on the planet.

Alas, for centuries, the Sacred Heart of Jesus has been co-opted into a private piety disconnected from the world, politics, and war — from the abyss of destruction. I have the impression that some uphold the image of the Sacred Heart of Jesus on the one hand, and the flag on the other, as if Jesus' personal salvation for us individually has nothing to do with what our country does, or how the poor suffer and die; as if we can worship the Sacred Heart, yet remain racist, sexist, greedy, selfish, violent, and warlike, as individuals and as a church and a nation.

I don't think we can truly honor the Sacred Heart of Jesus and at the same time support the war on Iraq, or the death penalty, or global warming, or corporate greed, or U.S. imperialism, or the School of the Americas, or the oppression of Palestinians, or the systematic oppression of Darfur and Haiti, or the development of nuclear weapons at Los Alamos. Or sit back in silence while these injustices rage.

Some conservative, right-wing Catholics like the image of the Sacred Heart and its personal implications, but they fail to let its nonviolent love unfold in concrete political policies and structures. Others on the more liberal side dismiss the image as a pious prop of the Catholic establishment instead of recognizing it as a call to plumb the mystical depths of universal love.

In any case, the heart of God beats on with a disarming, global love, awaiting our response, inviting us back from the abyss of destruction. The proof of our serious acceptance of this divine love will be nothing less than feeding the hungry, housing the homeless, educating all children in the methods of nonviolence, guaranteeing free health-care to all, cleaning up the earth, ending our wars, dismantling our weapons, and sharing our resources equally.

The Sacred Heart cancels out all violence. It offers perfect nonviolence. To honor it is to worship a God of nonviolence, to welcome that disarming love and to practice that same loving, universal nonviolence. If we dare live in that nonviolent love of Jesus and unpack its social, economic, and political implications for ourselves and the world, we will become instruments that help lead humanity back from the abyss of destruction. Nothing is more important.

CHAPTER 5

Resurrection!

A few years ago, Daniel Berrigan and I celebrated Easter in a New York park with a few Jesuit friends. We held a small liturgy and had a picnic. After reading a Gospel account of the resurrection, we sat a few moments in silence. Then I said, "I'm amazed that Jesus came back at all. He had been betrayed, denied, abandoned, arrested, jailed, tortured, and executed, and yet he came back peaceably, forgiving everyone generously, punishing no one. He didn't get angry at them — he proceeded to make them breakfast!"

"Part of me thinks," I added, "that if it were me, I wouldn't have wanted to come back at all. I would have been angry, hurt, and resentful. I would have wanted nothing to do with those former friends. I'd have nursed a grudge for a few thousand years before I came back!"

Dan smiled and said quietly, "Jesus didn't have a mean bone in his body."

Exactly. Jesus keeps on making peace, without any trace of resentment, anger, or bitterness. He forgives us, gives us his peace, and invites us again to join his life of love, nonviolence, and compassion. Amazing.

That's what my heart hears when I think of resurrection. I hear a summons to carry on the work for justice and peace, and to do so with as much love as I can muster. I hear a call to forgive, offer compassion, be nonviolent, resist injustice, and live life to the full.

Resurrection brings more than new clothes or Easter baskets. It means peace is stronger than war, justice stronger than injustice, compassion stronger than contempt. Resurrection means forgiveness surpasses resentment and reconciliation surpasses revenge. It means nonviolence wins out over violence — all contrary to the standards of conventional wisdom. In Dan's words, resurrection represents "the slight edge of life over death." Or, as Dr. King put it, "Truth crushed to earth shall rise again."

Resurrection — the vindication of nonviolence over violence — amid our bloody history proves that active nonviolence, steadfast service, and public peacemaking are the will of God. Note too that the resurrection was illegal. Jesus committed civil disobedience when he rose from the dead. The Roman soldiers guarded the tomb to make sure he stayed dead, but once again, Jesus broke the imperial laws of death.

The nonviolent Jesus has risen above injustice, poverty, and violence. He is risen despite war. Executed himself, he is risen from the death penalty. Christ is risen beyond the power of nuclear weapons, racism, sexism, starvation, global warming, and violence itself. Christ is risen above the culture of death. A bold announcement — and we're called to prove it. We prove it with the boldness of our own lives, our faith, our nonviolent resistance to the forces of death.

Which is to say, we must share the peacemaking life of the risen Jesus. We must confront death and its metaphors. For we too are headed for resurrection — our survival is already guaranteed. We're free to live beyond the culture of death. We're free to reject violence and poverty and war. We're free to confront the ROTC, Los Alamos, and the Pentagon. We're free to dismantle nuclear weapons.

We prove we're resurrection people by putting down our swords and beating them into plowshares. By loving our enemies. By carrying on Jesus' work of nonviolent resistance against systemic injustice. By speaking out against the insane U.S. war on Iraq. And by persisting despite the obstacles, the opposition, and the apparent futility, knowing that the outcome, in God's hands, is assured.

"I shall die, but that is all I shall do for death," the poet Edna St. Vincent Millay wrote long ago. Here is a clue about withholding our cooperation from death. We're free to live life to the full now, knowing that eternal life has already begun. We're free to resist the forces of death, renounce fear, and refuse to give in to despair.

"Life is on our side," Thomas Merton wrote to the Polish poet Czeslaw Milosz in 1959. "The silence and the cross of which we know are forces that cannot be defeated. In silence and suffering, in the heartbreaking effort to be honest in the midst of dishonesty (most of all our own dishonesty), in all these is victory. It is Christ in us who drives us through darkness to a light of which we have no conception and which can only be found by passing through apparent despair. Everything has to be tested. All relationships have to be tried. All loyalties have to pass through fire. Much has to be lost. Much in us has to be killed, even much that is best in us. But Victory is certain. The resurrection is the only light."

And so, despite these grim times, I remain hopeful. With my friends, I keep an eye on the long-haul view of things, on resurrection, salvation, and eternity. I trust that with the God of peace, all that I hope for is possible. And as Dan taught me long ago, the best way to be hopeful is by doing hopeful things.

I trust that one day wars will end, that more and more people will rise up and speak out, that as we share the cross of nonviolent resistance we will taste the resurrection in its concrete manifestations as signs of God's reign breaking through into a new culture of peace. I place my hope not in America or our weapons or our evil war-making, but in the risen Jesus, who greets each one of us with astonishing words: "Peace be with you."

I think he means it. Alleluia!

CHAPTER 6

The Common Ground of Interfaith Nonviolence

Before moving to New Mexico, I served for three years as director of the Fellowship of Reconciliation, the largest interfaith peace organization in the United States. Once I called a meeting of all the leaders of the various religious fellowships. For several days we gathered to share our stories, exchange our visions of peace, and plan new ways to pursue disarmament and justice together. We were Buddhists, Muslims, Jews, Hindus, Native Americans, Baha'i, Baptists, Presbyterians, Lutherans, Episcopalians, Catholics, Methodists, and Mennonites.

I will never forget those days. More than a conference or a meeting, it was a spiritual experience. As peace activists and seekers from various religious traditions, we sat around a table as friends sharing a similar spiritual journey to peace. We discovered that we stood on the common ground of nonviolence. To the delight of everyone, each religious activist explained how nonviolence was at the core of their tradition. We also heard how each one shared the same struggle to claim nonviolence in the face of massive opposition — within their own community.

Muslims explained that "Islam" means peace, that they are required to live at peace with others. Buddhists spoke of the way of compassion and respect toward all living beings. Jews spoke of the vision of Shalom, and Isaiah's call that we "beat swords into plowshares" and "study war no more." We Christians confessed that Jesus is nonviolent, that he called us to love our enemies, that he blessed peacemakers, that his last words before his martyrdom were "Put down the sword," and that his first words after his resurrection were "Peace be with you!"

I remember apologizing to the group for the failure of Christians to practice the nonviolence of Jesus, for Christian crusades past and present, for the heresy of the just-war theory, and for "Christian" government leaders who wage war and stockpile nuclear weapons in the name of the nonviolent Jesus.

In response, everyone confessed that their own tradition had also failed the summons of faith-based nonviolence. I was especially struck by the Buddhist leaders who said that Buddhists were some of the most violent people in the world, that the massacre of thousands of people in Sri Lanka in recent years has been led by Buddhists — often by monks — in the name of Buddha. (On other occasions, Thich Nhat Hanh and I have discussed this failure among our people, even though the vision of nonviolence is so clear in our respective traditions.) I realized then that we had all failed the wisdom of nonviolence.

But what was so heartening was the discovery that nonviolence is at the core of every religion, regardless of what the world says, or what religious bigotry, fundamentalism, and misconceptions have bred. At the heart of each major religion is the vision of peace, the ideal of a reconciled humanity, the way of compassion and love and justice, the fundamental truth of nonviolence.

Mahatma Gandhi was the first to point toward interfaith nonviolence. He broke new ground in so many ways, from fighting segregation in South Africa through satyagraha and nonviolent resistance, to leading a peaceful revolution against British imperialism in India. But he saw early on the equality of the world's religions because of the common ground of nonviolence. He later professed a vow of tolerance toward all religions and openness to the truth of nonviolence within each religion.

Recently I published a collection of Gandhi's spiritual writings on nonviolence. Over the years I read the entire ninety-five volumes of his collected writings, an amazing experience in itself. I was delighted to see the progress in his spiritual journey, as he formed a community ashram of nonviolence in South Africa and decided to hold communal, contemplative prayer services every morning and evening.

When he moved to India and saw again the deep hostility between Hindus and Muslims, he made interfaith nonviolence the core of his daily worship. Each day when his community gathered for prayer, they read excerpts from the Hindu and Muslim scriptures, from the Sermon on the

Mount and the Hebrew Bible. Then they sat in silence for forty-five minutes. They usually concluded with a hymn about the all-inclusive love that reconciles everyone, the love even for one's enemies. Forty years of interfaith, contemplative prayer transformed Gandhi into a universal spirit, a transformation that all the major religious scriptures hope for all of us.

To the end, however, Gandhi's interfaith nonviolence was a scandal. In January 1948, during the last four weeks of his life, he held an open prayer service every night in New Delhi at the Birla House. He received daily death threats, and during one of those services a bomb went off, just missing Gandhi. Finally, on January 30, as he was walking to a service, peacefully, carefully, mindfully walking the way of nonviolence, he was shot and killed by a Hindu fundamentalist who was angered by his association with Muslims.

At the time of his death, Gandhi was preparing to host a gathering of the International Fellowship of Reconciliation. Peacemakers of all faiths, including peace-movement leaders from the United States, were planning to fly to Gandhi's ashram in October 1948 to spend a week with him, discussing interfaith nonviolence.

"Religions are different roads converging to the same point," Gandhi once wrote. "What does it matter that we take different roads, so long as we reach the same goal? . . . I believe that, if only we could all read the scriptures of different faiths, we should find that they are at bottom all one and were all helpful to one another. . . . There will be no lasting peace on earth unless we learn not merely to tolerate but even to respect other faiths as our own."

As we learn from each other's religion, Gandhi discovered, we can help each other deepen in the faith of our own personal tradition. His critique of organized Christianity — that it rejected the nonviolence of Jesus and has become an imperial religion based on the Roman empire — has helped innumerable Christians return to the core teachings of Jesus, beginning with the Sermon on the Mount. Martin Luther King Jr. testified that Gandhi more than anyone else helped him to follow Christ.

Gandhi teaches us that we share a common spirituality of nonviolence. That leads me to conclude that nonviolence is a key to understanding not only the religious, social, political, economic, and spiritual dimensions of life, but also what it means to be human. Contrary to what most people think, I believe we were created to live nonviolently, to be at peace with one another and creation, and that it is possible for the whole human race to live together nonviolently. Indeed, it is our only hope if we are to survive.

The challenge therefore is to practice the contemplative, active, and prophetic nonviolence at the core of our respective traditions. For Christians, that means sitting daily with the God of peace, allowing God to disarm our hearts, letting God use us as instruments of God's disarming love, loving even our enemies, and taking up the cross of nonviolent resistance to injustice, as Jesus did.

If each of us can plumb the depths of nonviolence in our religious traditions, we will unleash the contemplative springs of nonviolence within us, and peace will blossom among us.

If we dare open our hearts to the wisdom of nonviolence in other religious traditions, as Gandhi did, we will discover not only that religion should not be a cause of war and division, but also that it can be a healing path toward unity, reconciliation, and global disarmament.

If we can appreciate the spiritualities of nonviolence flowing from other religions, we will deepen our own particular spirituality of nonviolence.

For the last twenty years, I have experienced the deepest multicultural and interfaith connections through my work in the peace movement. I have developed many friendships across cultural and religious boundaries because of our shared vision of nonviolence. This interfaith peacemaking sprang from the civil rights movement, when Dr. King called religious leaders to march with him to Selma. The friendship modeled between Dr. King, Rabbi Abraham Heschel, and Thich Nhat Hanh still bears good fruit in our world and exemplifies the journey we must all make.

As the world hangs on the brink of nuclear and environmental destruction, as we wage war in the name of religion, we need to explore the religious roots of nonviolence, just as Gandhi did. Perhaps then we will hear the call to disarm, to embrace one another as sisters and brothers, and to welcome the gift of peace that has been already given.

PART II

Nonviolence in Action

As we come to know the seriousness of the situation — the wars, the racism, the poverty, the nuclear weapons — we come to realize that things will not be changed simply by words or demonstrations. Rather it's a question of living one's life in a drastically different way.

DOROTHY DAY

When we are really honest with ourselves, we must admit that our lives are all that really belong to us. So it is how we use our lives that determines what kind of people we are. It is my deepest belief that only by giving our lives do we find life. I am convinced that the truest act of courage, the strongest act of humanity is to sacrifice ourselves for others in a totally nonviolent struggle for justice. To be human is to suffer for others. God help us to be human.

CÉSAR CHÁVEZ

CHAPTER 7

Sackcloth and Ashes

The high desert of New Mexico, where I live, is one of the most beautiful places in the country, with its red mesas, fields of sagebrush, Sangre de Cristo mountains, and endless turquoise sky. Recently I visited Bandelier National Monument, where the Anasazi Native Americans lived from the 1100s until the 1500s, hidden away in a spectacular canyon surrounded by high brown cliffs. They shared everything in common, cared for their children, and lived together in peace. Each day they ascended the highest cliff into a large niche and there worshipped the Creator. While St. Francis strove to teach nonviolence in Europe, these holy people had already cobbled together a community of nonviolence. The people are long gone now, but their peaceful spirit remains. One comes away knowing one has been to a genuine place of peace.

But today on the top of that same mountain, beyond the canyon, lies a dark contrast — Los Alamos, the most destructive place in the world. It is the birthplace of the bomb, where business is booming, where a new generation of nuclear weapons, against international treaties, is in the works.

The Bush administration's 2005 budget was the largest nuclear weapons budget in history, even though the Cold War is over and there is no other nuclear superpower. Along with New Mexico's Sandia Labs, Los Alamos is the largest nuclear-weapons laboratory in the world. My friends and I argue that those billions should be spent instead on schools, jobs, homes, health care, medicine for HIV/AIDS, environmental cleanup, and food for the starving masses. Almost half of all U.S. nuclear-warhead spending occurs within just sixty miles of Los Alamos, and more nuclear weapons are stored around Albuquerque than in any other single place in the world. For the next fifteen years, if not longer, Sandia Labs will be the only place in the United States where plutonium bomb cores (known as "pits") are manufactured. It also maintains the largest nuclear disposal site in the Southwest. The plan is to dump millions of drums and boxes of nuclear waste there in the next few decades.

The Bush administration sent hundreds of thousands of U.S. soldiers over 10,000 miles into the desert of Iraq to kill over 600,000 Iraqis, supposedly to find and dismantle a weapon of mass destruction. And now everyone knows that our government lied to us, that there never were any weapons of mass destruction in Iraq, and that the whole war was an effort by Bush, Cheney, Rumsfeld and company to steal Iraq's oil for our oil companies. In New Mexico, my friends and I have been saying to whoever will listen, "You're looking for weapons of mass destruction? You didn't find them in Iraq? We found them! They're right here in our backyard! You don't have to bomb New Mexico — just outlaw them, dismantle them, and pledge never to make one more nuclear weapon ever again."

We name these weapons of mass destruction as immoral, sinful, evil, and demonic, and call for an end to the production, development, and maintenance of these weapons.

Most employees at Los Alamos are churchgoers, so those of us who are Christian tell them that as followers of the nonviolent Jesus, we are forbidden to support war and commanded to "put down the sword" and "love our enemies." We can't serve both the God of peace and the false gods of nuclear weapons. We can't follow the nonviolent Jesus on the one hand, and work at Los Alamos, pay for Los Alamos, or support Los Alamos on the other hand. We can't participate in plans to destroy the planet. That is the ultimate blasphemy. God created the world in "seven days," and we snub God and threaten to blow it up in seven minutes.

Our country is in massive denial about Hiroshima. We have never dealt with it. Instead we ignore it and pretend it didn't happen. So when my friends and I go to Los Alamos, we try to look deeply at Hiroshima, to meditate on it, to see the evil we did, to name it as evil, to repent of this evil, and to recognize that every one of us has to take responsibility for it, that we can no longer be neutral or silent or quiet about it. As I reflect on Hiroshima, I realize we can no longer just try to be good with this much evil in our backyard. We have to speak out against this institutionalized evil; otherwise, our silence is complicity. We have to break through the culture of nuclear terrorism and the necessary silence that allows it to flourish.

Each year, on August 6, hundreds gather to commemorate two coinciding events. Our group gathers to celebrate the Transfiguration and to mourn the bombing of Hiroshima. The feast celebrates the day when Jesus exploded with the spiritual power of nonviolence, bringing humanity light and peace and the fullness of love. The dropping of the atomic bomb, on the other hand, vaporized 140,000 people in a flash. Three days later, we dropped another atomic bomb on Nagasaki. This was a complete and utter renunciation of the words uttered from the cloud: "This is my beloved Son. Listen to him." Dorothy Day called the atomic explosions "the anti-Transfiguration." A demonic light had been made, nonviolence rejected, and humanity's future all but foreclosed. We had consigned ourselves to limp along under the cloud of the bomb.

On August 5, 2006, several hundred attended a mass for peace and heard the Transfiguration story. "This is my beloved Son. Listen to him." And we recalled what Jesus had to say: "Love one another; love your neighbor; forgive one another; be as compassionate as God. Seek first God's reign and God's justice. Do unto others as you would have them do unto you. Put down the sword. Love your enemies."

Kathy Kelly joined us in 2006 and spoke to nearly five hundred people in Santa Fe about her missions of peace to Iraq and stressed the need to resist the war. Then, on August 6, we ascended Los Alamos in the spirit of resistance. Now with a different story — the story of Jonah, who urged the people of Nineveh to repent, a message, against the odds, that the people took to heart. Like them, we donned sackcloth, sat in ashes, and repented of the mortal sin of war and nuclear weapons. There in the heart of town, along Trinity and Oppenheimer Roads, we renounced our violence, our complicity. And we opened our hearts to God's gift of peace.

This creative action may seem odd, but as I said, it goes back thousands of years to the prophet Jonah, who called the people of Nineveh to conversion:

> The Word of God came to Jonah a second time: "Set out for the great city of Nineveh, and announce to it the message that I will tell you." So Jonah made ready and went to Nineveh, according to the Lord's bidding. Now Nineveh was an enormously large city; it took three days to

go through it. Jonah began his journey through the city, and had gone but a single day's walk announcing, "Forty days more and Nineveh shall be destroyed," when the people of Nineveh believed God. They proclaimed a fast, and all of them, great and small, put on sackcloth. When the news reached the king of Nineveh, he rose from his throne, laid aside his robe, covered himself with sackcloth, and sat in ashes. Then he had this proclaimed throughout Nineveh, by decree of the king and his nobles: "Neither humans nor beasts, neither cattle nor sheep, shall taste anything. They shall not eat, nor shall they drink water. People and animals shall be covered with sackcloth and call loudly to God. Everyone shall turn from their evil ways and from the violence they have in hand. Who knows, God may relent and forgive, and withhold blazing wrath, so that we shall not perish." When God saw by their actions how they turned from their evil way, God repented of the evil that God had threatened to do to them. God did not carry it out. (Jonah 3:1-10)

This tale is perhaps the only episode in the Hebrew scriptures where the political leader and the entire people actually stopped their violence and committed themselves to peace. In the Gospel of Luke, Jesus affirmed that act of repentance when he suggested that the people of Chorazin and Bethsaida should repent in sackcloth and ashes like the people of Nineveh (Luke 10:13-14).

If Jonah and Jesus thought that the people of Nineveh, Chorazin, and Bethsaida should repent in sackcloth and ashes, what would they think about Los Alamos?

A few days after the bombing of Hiroshima and Nagasaki, Gandhi said flatly, "The atom bomb brought an empty victory to the Allied armies. It resulted for the time being in destroying Japan. What has happened to the soul of the destroying nation is yet too early to see."

We as a people are losing our soul because of our commitment to these weapons of mass destruction. So my friends and I go to Los Alamos to remember Hiroshima, work to make sure it never happens again, and in the process regain our souls.

On that August day of 2006, the symbols of Jonah's story converged and enlightened. The ashes reminded us of the ash of Hiroshima. Jonah reminded us of the ancient city of Nineveh, today known as Mosul in Iraq, which the United States shattered and poisoned with depleted uranium.

There have been only a handful of protests or observances of Hiroshima Day at Los Alamos since the 1940s. The media has granted our protest some attention. The church balks at our politically charged prayer. Even the government has noticed. The governor of New Mexico even met with us to discuss our demand for disarmament.

Such a strange way to pass a quiet afternoon — itching in sackcloth, dusty with ashes, anti-war signs in our hands. And this in a town of thousands of intellectuals busy making weapons of mass destruction and getting paid handsomely for their trouble. The contrast boggles the mind.

I sat silently along Trinity Road with the others, trying to stay mindful, to enter the spirit of the moment. And in silence I apologized to God for the violence I've committed — against myself, my friends and relatives, my fellow church people. I apologized for doing too little to disarm violence. I apologized for loving none too well my sisters and brothers around the world. A humbling experience, but one offering a consolation of sorts. Repentance brings inner peace.

We did what we could. We offered our prayers, pledged to keep at it, and said our piece along these lines: Our government's weapons are immoral, unjust, impractical, illegal, criminal, idolatrous, sinful, and demonic. They don't protect us; they don't make us safer. They are the ultimate form of terrorism. They are blasphemous before the Creator. And they are larcenous. The billions spent on them rob the world's poor.

We also had a thing or two to say to the good people of the town. Quit your jobs and be converted to the nonviolent Christ. You cannot serve the God of peace and the false gods of war. You cannot love your enemies as you design the means to vaporize them. You cannot follow the nonviolent Jesus and maintain a nuclear arsenal.

One wonders if they heard. But such is never the cardinal issue. The true efficacy of the weekend lay in our own broken hearts. Urged by one another, consoled in the silence, we pledged anew to take Jesus at his word. We resolved to follow him on the road to peace and practice his way of creative nonviolence. To go so far as the cross in the hopes of a transfigured world, a world without war, poverty, or nuclear weapons. Such a world as the Anasazi people created long ago.

31

CHAPTER 8

Standing Up at the School of the Americas

Each year around November 16, nearly twenty thousand people gather at Fort Benning, Georgia, outside the gates of the notorious "School of the Americas." The school has trained some sixty-four thousand Central and South Americans, many of whom have gone on to commit murder and torture as members of Latin American death squads — a sinister distinction that has earned the place the more infamous title of "School of Assassins." The yearly protests are by now as rooted as the Georgia pines and have the Pentagon on the defensive. The Pentagon's first official response was a PR move. A name change came down. They now call the place "The Western Hemisphere Institute for Security Cooperation."

The name has changed, but nothing else. The place still trains the aristocracy's thugs to brutalize the campesinos. There soldiers enroll in such courses as "Counterinsurgency," "Psychological Warfare," "Military Intelligence," and "Interrogation Tactics." There soldiers study how to target Latin American educators, union organizers, catechists, student leaders, human rights workers, priests, and nuns.

Latin American soldiers learn how to arrest, torture, and behead. They learn how to stealthily assassinate a solitary target and massacre dozens in a village. To learn the art of killing, the SOA is the place to go.

I've gone to protest four times already and was arrested with thousands of others in 1998 and 1999. But why go again? What good comes of it? I keep going for several reasons.

"Every known terrorist training camp must be shut down," said George W. Bush. I go to demand just that. Let the SOA be the first one to close. Immoral, inhuman, illegal, demonic — this terrorist school has no right to exist. It's part and parcel of the web of lies, murders, and massacres that the U.S. inflicts in Iraq every day. The SOA brings no democracy to our sisters and brothers in Latin America. It brings only death. A truly democratic institution would ensure the well-being of every adult and child through only nonviolent methods. A school promoting democracy would teach nonviolence and proudly embrace the name "Institute of Nonviolent Cooperation."

I'll go again because these days it trains the death squads who kill farmers, teachers, and activists in Colombia. The blood of the poor stains the hands of the death squads, soldiers, paramilitaries, politicians, and U.S. advisors — all trained and their actions orchestrated by the United States at the SOA.

I'll go to the SOA protest because it's one of the best organized and more hopeful events in the church and the country. And it's one of the best examples of active nonviolence in our history. In addition, it is beautiful and urgent liturgy. Its founder, my friend Father Roy Bourgeois, and his team took the movement directly to South America this year and convinced the governments of Venezuela, Argentina, Uruguay, and Bolivia not to send their troops to Georgia. And pressure grows in Congress for legislation that will put the SOA out of business.

I'll go again to the SOA protest because Jesus himself was a victim of arrest, imprisonment, and torture. And he died at the hands of imperial death squads. As one trying to be his follower, I want to side with him as he sides with the victims of the U.S. empire around the world — from El Salvador to Colombia to Iraq.

And I'll go to the SOA protest because I'm haunted by Ignacio Ellacuría and the other Jesuit martyrs of El Salvador. I worked with them for several months in 1985, four years before they were assassinated. They sent me and a few other young U.S. Jesuits to work in harassed refugee camps. Death squads lurked about, and on the occasions they approached, I went out to greet them. There was a rationale behind the plan. Perhaps the conspicuous presence of a North American would avert violence.

And so when they appeared, I hauled my trembling bones to the gate. All the while U.S. aircraft crisscrossed the sky and unleashed bombs in the near distance. Through my fear I managed to learn a thing or two about faith, hope, and love. It was the suffering people, and most of all the steadfast Jesuits, who taught me best.

Said Father Ellacuría, renowned theologian, philosopher, and university president: "The purpose of UCA [the Jesuit university in El Salvador] is to promote the reign of God. But we have learned that if you want to promote the reign of God, you have to stand up publicly, actively, against the anti-reign. You can no longer say you are for peace and justice unless you publicly, actively stand up against war and injustice. You can no longer claim to pursue the good, unless you are publicly, actively resisting systemic, institutionalized, structured evil."

His insight profoundly moved me. It sounded like a new morality for a new millennium. It turns out it's what Gandhi had taught decades earlier: "Noncooperation with evil is as much a duty as cooperation with good."

And they held on to it, come what may. On November 16, 1989, in the middle of the night, twenty-eight soldiers, nineteen of them trained at the SOA, burst in upon the Jesuits, shot up their house, and forced them outside. They laid the Jesuits on the ground and shot them dead. Then they removed their brains. It was "to send a message," said Jon Sobrino, a Jesuit who survived by virtue of his being in Thailand. "It was to say to all of Latin America — 'This is what you get if you *think* about reality.'"

The Jesuits' steadfast spirit, fearless determination, and strong faith still inspire me. I think of them every day. And so I go to the SOA to carry on their great work, to think about reality, to name the destruction of the poor carried out by our nation. I go gratefully on this anniversary of their murders.

CHAPTER 9

To the Tombs and Back

On January 16, 2001, sixteen of us were arrested for standing in front of the doorway to the U.S. Mission at the United Nations on First Avenue in New York City. We were honoring Dr. King's birthday and commemorating the tenth anniversary of the Gulf War massacre. After a brief prayer service featuring the meager daily food rations that Iraqis suffer, we walked to the entranceway, held signs calling for an end to the sanctions on Iraq, and sang songs of peace. Within minutes we were handcuffed and hauled off. But what appeared to be a small, symbolic gesture, ridiculed or ignored by passersby, quickly became a profound experience.

I have been arrested in New York City for opposing war and injustice perhaps twenty times since 1984, but rarely have I landed all the way at the bottom of the barrel like we did this winter day. Mayor Giuliani had recently announced that anyone arrested in New York City, no matter how minor the charge, would go through the system.

So began our journey down into the Tombs, the ancient prison down in the bowels of the city. We met all kinds of people. An elderly Muslim man who worked as a subway-token distributor, accused of stealing. Two young people picked up for selling Superbowl T-shirts without a permit. Several accused of selling drugs or being in the company of people using drugs. All of them had to go through the system. So did we.

First we sat for hours in the local precinct holding cell on 57th Street. It seemed like another case of "rounding up the usual suspects," who included longtime peace activists like Kathy Kelly of Voices in the Wilderness, Sisters Ardeth Platte and Carol Gilbert of Jonah House, Richard Deats of the Fellowship of Reconciliation, Karl Meyer of the Catholic

Worker and Peace House, and my great Jesuit brothers Simon Harak and Daniel Berrigan.

The eight of us men sat crowded together in a stinking, filthy cell, without any food until late in the evening. Then the police handcuffed us together, connecting each of us with two feet of stainless-steel chain, and marched us out at one A.M. into the bitter cold. Hunched together in the back of a police van, we were driven to Central Booking at 100 Center Street, where everyone arrested in Manhattan is eventually brought.

A new TV show was premiering that same night called "100 Center Street," full of the adventures of New York's hardworking police, lawyers, and judges as they send people to this dungeon. They should call the show by the more common name for this place, "The Tombs."

That day more than five hundred people had been arrested on the streets of New York, making it the most crowded Tuesday night in the Tombs ever, as far as any jailer could remember.

At two A.M. we were led by our chains down a street to wait in the freezing night air to enter the Tombs. But they were full. So we were led back down the street, to sit and freeze for an hour and a half in the back of a police van. Finally, by 3:30 A.M., we were brought in, where they took mug shots, searched us, and interviewed us. Eventually we were locked into another small cell.

What an experience to be chained to your friends in the freezing cold, escorted at night by armed guards along the streets of New York, and then led slowly, precariously down endless stairwells to some dark, dingy prison cell, like a Roman slave dungeon.

In an instant your faith, stamina, nonviolence, and spirituality are tested. You quickly find out how strong your spirit is, not to mention your body. In an instant the Gospel of Jesus, the Acts of the Apostles, and the letters of St. Paul come alive, with their stories of jail, guards, and prisons.

The jailers laughed and joked with one another, and generally seemed to have a good time while doing their police duty. In fact, on the whole they appeared to be fairly considerate to people. And yet they oversaw one of the most inhuman places in the country.

Once we hit rock bottom, we saw around us a vast array of crowded jail cells, full of hundreds of African-Americans and Latinos. Our fellow prisoners were tired, anxious, frustrated, and probably scared, knowing that they would most likely be sent on immediately to nearby Riker's Island, the largest prison in the world, located near LaGuardia Airport.

Throughout the day my friends and I tried to cheer each other up, share our stories, describe our work, and tell hilarious jokes. For most of the day there were ten of us in a small cell, sitting against the wall, with room for one or two to stretch out on the dirty floor.

In particular, our friend and hero, Daniel Berrigan, in his eighties, endured this ordeal with great grace, sitting for long stretches like Buddha, never complaining, telling jokes, reminiscing about his imprisonment in Danbury. We had just been celebrating Phil Berrigan's release from a Maryland prison.

When the baloney sandwich came at eleven A.M., all I could do was eat the Wonder Bread. There was nothing else to eat, nothing to drink, nothing to read; we endured bright lights, loud noise, and endless harassment. Every hour or two the jailers pushed us all into one or two big cells and reassigned new cells to us as different people were called to appear upstairs before a judge. By the afternoon, my friends and I were exhausted and getting sick.

Finally, at five P.M., we were brought upstairs to stand before a judge. We pled not guilty. A trial date was set. We were released back onto the cold streets of New York.

We had been through a terrible ordeal, twenty-nine crushing hours in the System, in the Tombs. I was tired, hungry, nauseous, exhausted, and not sure if I could have made it one more day.

And yet that was the whole point: This is what life is like every day, not just for the disenfranchised of New York City but for the children of Iraq.

During the '90s, over one million Iraqis, mostly children under five, died because of our sanctions. Most of those children were born long after the Gulf War. Saddam Hussein did not kill them with poisonous water, malnutrition, or the destruction of Iraq's basic infrastructure. No, our government killed them and continues to kill them.

Every day is like a day in the Tombs for the children of Iraq. They are consigned to death.

Throughout our ordeal, our prayer was for the children of Iraq. When asked by jailers or other prisoners, we told the story of the dying Iraqi children. To a person, they understood.

Coming up from the Tombs, gasping for fresh air, in the end we felt grateful. Grateful for the opportunity to take a stand on behalf of the suffering Iraqi children. Grateful to taste the daily life inflicted on the disenfranchised and imprisoned. Grateful to understand anew what Jesus endured, what the Gospel calls us to risk for the sake of justice and peace.

Once again we realized the truth of the Beatitudes: "Blessed are you when people abuse you and persecute you and speak all kinds of calumny against you on my account. Rejoice and be glad."

CHAPTER 10

The Santa Fe Nine

"We're here to collect Senator Pete Domenici's signature on 'The Declaration of Peace,' a national campaign to end the U.S. war on Iraq," we said to the security official in the lobby of the Santa Fe Federal Building. "We're here to collect his promise that from now on he will work to end this immoral, evil war and bring the troops home, and pursue reparations and nonviolent solutions for the Middle East."

It was September 26, 2006. The guards stared in disbelief. They knew that New Mexico's senator is one of the Bush administration's biggest supporters, one of the greatest defenders of nuclear weapons in history. We knew it too. When some of our group wrote and asked him to oppose the Iraq war, he wrote a letter in return — a letter brimming with braggadocio and punctuated by boasts of his support for the war. We responded in turn by deciding to take a stand for peace — or, more specifically, a sit-in for peace.

It was part of a nationwide plan. That week, some 375 actions took place against the Bush administration's war on Iraq. Thousands of signers of the Declaration of Peace pledged to pressure their Congressional representatives to vote against Bush's war on Iraq. Over 250 people were arrested in acts of civil disobedience, from the White House to the Los Angeles Federal Building. No one read about it in *The New York Times*, but it happened, and it generated new hope. I think it helped spark Democratic candidates across the country to speak out against the war and turn the tide in the 2006 congressional elections that November.

Our own action was modest, but beautiful. For the first time in thirty-five years, according to local police, Santa Fe witnessed civil disobedience.

Nine of us entered the federal building and made our request. We were promptly denied entrance, kept walking anyway, and got as far as the elevator before the police stopped us. They pulled the plug on the elevator, with the doors still open, and there we conducted our protest.

Earlier that week I had printed out from several Web sites the name of every U.S. soldier killed in Iraq over the last few years, plus about ten thousand names of innocent Iraqi civilians. And there in the elevator we started reading those names aloud, first from the list of Americans, then from the list of Iraqis, alternating back and forth. Our voices carried to everyone in the lobby, until eventually the police forced the lobby closed.

Among us the litany of the dead hit home. It was sobering. Some began to weep. All of us bowed our heads in silent prayer as the names poured forth — the precious names of the squandered and brutalized from an immoral, illegal, and unnecessary war. Here was a lamentation, a prayer of intercession, a cold, hard look at the consequences of our pursuit of Iraq's oil. The reading went on for six hours.

The nine of us, cramped on the elevator floor, came from all walks of life — a fifteen-year-old student, a retired librarian, several radical feminists, a disabled elderly man. All of us were trying to take a stand for peace.

Congregating close by was a large contingent of the Santa Fe police force, FBI agents, a SWAT team, federal marshals, and Homeland Security officials, waiting and observing, hearing our litany. We read on and on and held our ground. Outside, scores kept vigil, the media hovered about, and frustrated politicians passed by. Finally, around five o'clock, the Homeland Security officials moved in and escorted us from the building and issued citations. One year later we finally stood trial and were found guilty. I was sentenced to six months' supervised probation.

A small gesture, to be sure. And though it might seem futile, actions just like ours have made all the difference in our nation's history. From the abolitionists and the suffragists to the labor and civil rights movements to the anti-war movements, from the Boston Tea Party to Rosa Parks and the Berrigans, history shows that when good people cross the line and break the law and take a risk for justice and peace, positive social change happens. In other words, when we enter the Paschal Mystery, when we risk the cross as nonviolent resistance to systemic, institutional injustice, a breakthrough occurs.

I think we've entered into Orwell's nightmare of a postmodern, post-Christian era of permanent war. We have a president who champions war, a Congress that writes blank checks for war, an enthralled media that trumpets war, a sheepish citizenry that lets itself get fleeced for war, churches that confer their blessings on war, and courts that legalize weapons and imprison those who say no to war. Our war isn't only permanent but universal — we make war on the poor, on children, on the earth, on humanity, on God.

But complaining does no good, and it's not an authentic Christian response anyway. The Christian response to a "surge of war" is a counter-surge of peace, a swell of peacemakers and nonviolent resisters. All of us need to stand up, join some public action, get involved with our local peace group, speak out, and on occasion sit in. With every act of peace, the unanimity of the status quo unravels and hope resurges. And we show ourselves disciples of the nonviolent Jesus.

Sitting in and standing up for peace goes all the way back to Jesus. I wrote about it in my book *The Sacrament of Civil Disobedience*. Jesus, I wrote, was a one-man crime wave. In his passionate pursuit of justice and equality, he committed dozens of acts of nonviolent civil disobedience. His final one — turning over the tables of injustice in the Temple and calling for contemplative prayer — stands as his culminating instance of dramatic, symbolic nonviolent action — his clearest, most poignant, best-aimed gesture, a gesture aimed at the heart of Judean-Roman imperial power. It was the action that cost him his life.

His example rings true today. Paying up is part and parcel of the Christian's job description. We're supposed to take up the cross of nonviolent resistance against the empire of war, and to accept the consequences. After all, the person we follow suffered arrest, an abusive stint in jail, brutality and torture, and finally execution. Such is the path for his followers, the way of daring nonviolence with all of its risks.

In our own days of war and poverty and nuclear weapons, we must take risks through our own actions of creative nonviolence. And we must keep taking them until the war ends, hunger is eradicated, and nuclear weapons are abolished. We must keep on walking the road to peace.

CHAPTER 11

Generosity, Not Domination

A few years ago my friend Rabbi Michael Lerner of *Tikkun* magazine launched the Network of Spiritual Progressives, a group I joined, to unite religious activists from across the spectrum to confront the issues dividing the nation and the world. In 2007 we placed an ad in *The New York Times* entitled "An Ethical Way to End the War in Iraq: Generosity Beats Domination as a Strategy for Homeland Security." It sparked immediate debate and serious interest from many politicians about a new way forward.

Our statement outlines three basic steps. First, we agree that the war is wrong and that we undertake repentance with renewed generosity toward the world's poor. "The remedy for wrongdoing begins not only with the act of changing the path (stop funding the war) but also with apology and repentance. Therefore we ask that our elected representatives go before the U.N. and acknowledge that it was wrong for the U.S. to invade Iraq, that hundreds of thousands of innocent people have been killed and wounded in the chain of events that our invasion precipitated. The war has also created over two million refugees. For the suffering and deaths that have come from this invasion, we, the American people, ask forgiveness."

As we do this, we acknowledge our fundamental mistake — that "safety and security can be achieved through domination or control of others" — and assert instead "that a better path to safety and security is to treat others with generosity, kindness, and genuine concern for their well-being. We urge the Congress to pass a resolution rejecting the strategy of domination and embracing the strategy of generosity, and calling upon the world's people to forgive our society for the destructive path it has followed."

Second, our statement recommends replacing U.S. and British forces in

Iraq with an international peace force acceptable to the Iraqi people, composed primarily of Muslims from non-neighboring states and also non-Muslims from other states not engaged in violence or economic boycotts against the Iraqi people. It further recommends providing security and conducting a plebiscite so that the Iraqi people themselves can determine their future. "The U.S. should give all our Iraqi military bases to this force, leave no forces behind as 'advisors' or deployed in neighboring states ready to re-intervene, and we should require all U.S. corporations operating in Iraq to give at least the majority of their Iraq-derived profits to the task of Iraqi reconstruction."

Third, our statement recommends rebuilding Iraq and launching a global Marshall Plan. The United States must commit hundreds of billions of dollars to fully rebuild Iraq. But that is only part of a larger global Marshall Plan that the United States should now announce — "to commit at least one percent of the Gross Domestic Product (GDP) of the U.S. each year for the next twenty years toward the goals of eliminating global and domestic poverty, homelessness, inadequate health care, inadequate education, and of repairing the environment."

The statement continues, "Just as the first Marshall Plan allocated 1.5-2% of GDP after the Second World War to the rebuilding of Europe, this second Marshall Plan, extended to the rest of the world, will provide far more homeland security for the U.S. than the currently planned military spending that will squander our resources."

This global Marshall Plan, suggests Rabbi Lerner, is the beginning of a new strategy of generosity, a core requirement of our scriptures, which can help recreate new levels of trust. It not only helps increase American security and respect for America around the world, but it is also morally appropriate and religiously mandated. "Fostering an ethos of genuine caring for others — countering the ethos of selfishness, materialism, and me-firstism that has been the 'common sense' of a cynical media and our market-driven culture — must become the highest domestic and foreign policy priority for our society."

The statement continues, "Don't let media and politicians convince you this is 'unrealistic' or 'utopian,' because history shows (and the Iraq war proves) that militarism and domination are far less 'realistic' as paths to peace and security."

My friends and I keep hope in such a practical vision, a new national conversion of heart that produces concrete change, beginning with the end of this immoral, illegal, evil war and the elimination of poverty, disease, and nuclear weapons, which are at the root of terrorism.

Violence, war, and domination have utterly failed to achieve any noble end. Let's try God's commandment of universal love, through active disarmament and global generosity. We might one day discover what true peace looks like.

PART III

Pilgrimages of Nonviolence

Peacemaking belongs to the heart of our Christian vocation. Peacemaking is a full-time task for all Christians. Peacemaking has become in our century the most urgent of all Christian tasks.

HENRI NOUWEN

Practicing nonviolence is first of all to become nonviolence. Then when a difficult situation presents itself, we will react in a way that will help the situation.

THICH NHAT HANH

CHAPTER 12

A Pilgrimage to Gandhi's India

Saturday, 25 December 2004, Galway, Ireland

It's Christmas Day, and I'm in Galway on the west coast of Ireland, staying with my friend Terry Howard, S.J., after visiting other Jesuit friends in Dublin, and Mairead Maguire and her family near Belfast. It's cold, quiet, and wet, but beautiful and refreshing to be here, to celebrate the coming of the God of peace into our world. Terry and I drove along the coast for a few hours, looking out at the Aran Islands, then joined the Jesuit community for Christmas mass and dinner.

This is just a brief stop on my way to India. I have dreamed of going to India since I was a boy. One night when I was five, I had a vivid dream about traveling through this land. I told my older brother about it when I woke up. It has haunted me ever since. I always presumed that one day my dream would come true.

My interest in India has grown steadily over the decades as I have studied and pondered the life of Mahatma Gandhi. He remains for me the most significant peacemaker of the last century. I was greatly affected by the 1982 movie about him, began to study his life, and then, like him, professed a vow of nonviolence in 1984. Reading the ninety-five volumes of his collected works a few years ago made a deep impression on me.

Now I'm on my way to India, with a "Global Exchange" tour led by my friend Arun Gandhi, Gandhi's grandson, who lives in Memphis and teaches nonviolence around the world. I go to India as a pilgrim in search of God and truth, to listen and learn about India and Gandhi, to meet the good people who are implementing his vision and constructive programs, and to deepen my own commitment to nonviolence. May the suffering people of India break open my heart and teach me anew the lessons of peace. I go with eyes wide open, including the third one.

Sunday, 26 December 2004, Dublin, Ireland

Sometime around eight A.M. this morning, an earthquake measuring 9.1 on the Richter scale struck under the Indian Ocean about 190 kilometers off Sumatra, Indonesia, setting off enormous forty-foot tidal waves that struck India, Indonesia, Sri Lanka, Bangladesh, Burma, Thailand, and even Somalia. We watched the first news reports before driving back to Dublin. No one knows how many were swept out to sea. First estimates say thirty thousand people are dead. I am overwhelmed with grief and sorrow. Lord, have mercy on them all. It is hard to believe that I am on my way to India the day after this disaster.

Tonight, Terry and I had dinner with our friend Jim Corkery, S.J., in one of the Dublin Jesuit communities. Everyone is shaken by the news.

Monday, 27 December 2004, London, England

I flew to London this morning for a layover before tomorrow's six A.M. flight to Bombay. I spent the day walking around town, from Piccadilly and Leicester Square to Regent's Park and St. John's Wood.

I grieve the shocking loss of life from the tsunami. I grieve the arrogance, violence, and stupidity of the Bush administration, wreaking havoc on the world, bringing a veritable tsunami of violence and death to Iraqis, Palestinians, and Afghanis, and not lifting a finger to help the suffering people of Darfur, Haiti, and Colombia. Life is so precious and fragile, what with tidal waves, earthquakes, hurricanes, and fires. Why do we have to bring so much pain to so many people around the world? Life is hard enough without our wars and injustices. Instead, we should spend our resources relieving pain, feeding the world, and protecting people from every natural disaster.

Tuesday, 28 December 2004, Mumbai, India

The tone of my Gandhian pilgrimage has changed with this disaster. I feel shocked, appalled, worried, and sad. As I waited for the flight at Heathrow, scores of bedraggled people got off flights from Asia. The news had been reporting that survivors from the Thai resorts hit by the tsunami were beginning to return. I feel helpless and powerless in the face of this natural disaster, but as I fly across Turkey, Iran, and Pakistan, I am determined again to listen. I go to India not as a fan of Gandhi, not to idolize him, but to see India through his eyes and to hear the wisdom of nonviolence. Maybe, just maybe, some of Gandhi's nonviolence will rub off and inspire me for the journey ahead.

I saw Richard Rohr last week in Albuquerque, and he said he had visited India earlier this year for the first time. "You will not be the same after India," he said. "Everyone is changed by India." He told me that after seeing such widespread poverty and powerlessness, he could never be impatient again.

Bombay is now called Mumbai, and I stepped into ninety-degree humidity outside the airport to be greeted by someone from the tour group. There was a mob of people and a sea of auto rickshaws, three-wheeled, covered golf carts that serve as taxis. I immediately felt at home and knew I would love it. We drove across Mumbai through the terrible eleven P.M. traffic and passed by shacks and shops on the way to Juhu Beach, where the group was gathering.

Wednesday, 29 December 2004

I spent the day resting before meeting with the tour group tonight. I feel a great sense of relief just being out of the United States, away from its arrogance, imperialism, greed, and indifference. It is refreshing and sobering to stand with the people of India, to witness their poverty, to meet their dignity and courage, and to realize once again that there is more to life than George W. Bush's America.

Reports now say that sixty-five thousand people died in the tsunami and that the number will rise dramatically. I mourn for them and pray for them all, and try to grasp the magnitude and meaning of this event.

I went for a walk along the beautiful Juhu Beach, where Gandhi used to rest after his fasts and imprisonments, but I was immediately accosted by several starving mothers holding their babies and about twenty girls, all wearing rags. They were touching me, holding me, and pleading for money. They surrounded me, so I left. Along the way I saw homeless beggars, speeding taxis and auto rickshaws, palm trees and the ocean. I realized that I felt at home because I had seen this before — in San Salvador, Guatemala City, Manila, Port-au-Prince, and Managua. I recognized this poverty. India is filled with pain, grief, sorrow, destitution, and unspeakable poverty. It is an indictment of the Rich World's greed, selfishness, and injustice. What is so different about India for me is the sheer size of it. I have never seen so many people, most of them terribly poor.

India is one third the size of the United States, with three times the population — over 1.1 billion people. Forty percent of its population are under fifteen years old. About 70 percent live — and die — in some six hundred thousand villages.

Tonight, Arun Gandhi welcomed the group and gave an introductory talk about Gandhi, our trip, and India's poverty. He explained that Gandhi urged India to develop the villages and figure out simple, sustainable cottage industries so that the poor could survive. India rejected his vision and industrialized the cities. Then many villagers moved there, and now the problems are immense. Gandhi's dream remains the only viable solution: a return to simple village life and a national program to support village sustainability.

Thursday, 30 December 2004

I woke to the news that one hundred thousand people have now been declared dead from the tsunami. Entire villages have vanished. Millions are injured or homeless. Unbelievable. Unimaginable. God have mercy on the dead and the survivors and us all.

Then I watched in disbelief as the United States offered to contribute $15 million for disaster relief. I am speechless and appalled by this cold, callous offer. What an insult to India, Indonesia, Sri Lanka, and Southeast Asia! Bush is about to spend $50 million on his inauguration party. Last year he spent $150 billion to kill one hundred thousand Iraqis, and he plans to spend another $100 billion this year. Yet he refuses to offer any serious aid to the millions hurt by the tidal waves. On Christmas Day, Bush called the American people to be more compassionate. But when the tsunami hit, he remained on vacation in Texas all week. He symbolizes the coldhearted hypocrisy of the Rich World. We fund killing people, not saving people. Instead, we should take the war funds and spend that $100 billion on tsunami relief, spend it on water, food, medicine, and shelters, and then work to eliminate hunger and disease everywhere.

But the slaughter of Iraq goes on. Dozens were killed in Baghdad these last few days. The only bright spot is the news of Yushchenko's election in the Ukraine, thanks to the thousands of nonviolent resisters who shut down the country demanding re-election.

After breakfast our group drove all morning out of the city into the countryside, passing thousands of shacks, barefoot children, women in saris, and auto rickshaws. At one point, as we waited at a crowded intersection, a three-year-old boy stood holding his father's hand for five minutes, waving at us with a huge smile. So happy, at peace, full of joy, in the midst of poverty. He was blessing us.

We spent the day at the Women's Indian Trust, a women's program where they empower women to rebuild their lives, train them to work, and help them get their own homes. They spin cloth, print materials, make clothes, and produce children's toys. They also manage a day care and a crafts shop. These women confront India's long history of patriarchy. Traditionally, men do not allow women to leave home. But here women take responsibility for themselves. (This program should be replicated throughout India. It's just like the Sacred Heart Center in Richmond, Virginia, which I used to direct.) We spent time visiting their nursing training program, where they teach local women the basics of health care and then send them into the slums and the countryside. Before lunch we visited the child-care section and the school.

$$* \qquad * \qquad *$$

I believe the tsunami tragedy was preventable. During the last century the world spent $20 trillion to kill 170 million people in wars. If we never went to war and used that money instead for human resources, we could wipe out hunger, disease, and poverty. We could clean up the environment and improve life for billions. With the extra money left over, we could set up a global tsunami warning system — which was not in place here — to get people out before the waves arrive. Sri Lanka had two hours before the wave struck. Everyone could have been moved inland within fifteen minutes; thousands could have been saved. We could also improve our earthquake, tornado, and hurricane warning systems. But life is cheap. We do not care for the world's poor — only for corporate profits.

It is embarrassing to see Bush and Powell on the news. A U.N. official announced the day after the tragedy that the rich nations were being "stingy." Powell angrily denied that. Indian TV is more respectful, sensitive, mournful, and attentive to the reality of suffering.

Friday, 31 December 2004

The morning paper states that over 125,000 people are now confirmed dead from the tsunami. Meanwhile, Bush gave an angry speech against the U.N. official, saying that the United States is "not stingy," that it is a "kind-hearted, generous nation." He increased the tsunami aid to all of $35 million, still not even the amount he is spending for his inauguration party. What a scandal and an affront to the rest of the world! It is so painful to see U.S. arrogance and selfishness. We are the Scrooge of the world. This morning our group visited the poorest slums of Mumbai and a Gandhian project called "The Marketplace," led by a group of women who run simple programs to empower other women and children in the slums by forming cooperatives to make and sell crafts. The poverty is overwhelming, with the dogs, sewage, trash, shacks, and pollution. When we walked through the endless, narrow, tunnel-like stone alleys between the crowded shacks, I felt I was back in Cité Soleil in Haiti or Guatemala City.

But the women are great. Though they are poor, they have selflessly given their lives to other poor women. They are true models of kindness, compassion, and generosity — everything Bush claims for himself and the American empire, everything he and First-World America are not. He could learn from them the meaning of compassion and generosity. "Empowerment for poor women," one of the women explains to us, "begins by getting food so they can eat. Only then can they begin to work and earn an income." It was scary for these women to take a stand and join the cooperative. They are courageous.

We spent several hours listening to their testimonies, how they learned to stitch, organize cooperatives, and manage to support themselves. They make all the decisions themselves. They clean up the slums. They promote good hygiene. They also teach interreligious dialogue, respect toward others, and parenting skills. They offer vacation programs for children and support groups for teenagers. Nearly five hundred women are involved in these programs. As we walked through the endless alleyways, I was overwhelmed by the poverty, which was like a prison for half a million people, but these women give me hope. They are full of life and determination.

We spent time in one slum house that was a room about eight feet square with eight people living in it. It reminded me of the jail cell I shared with Philip Berrigan, of the family I stayed with in Palestine whose home was destroyed, who were given a cell by neighboring families. Everyone is unemployed, illiterate, and sick. But the children smile and laugh. Through this program they share their resources, clean their alleys, and look after one another.

This poverty is unimaginable. No human being should live like this. Bush should see it. Everyone in the United States should know about it. This is structural injustice, immorality, institutionalized evil. Where are the parks, the clean water systems, the large family rooms, the kitchens, the food, the doctors, the schools, and the sports fields? How do they survive? They don't. They suffer early and unjust deaths, and the world looks the other way. Yet these women have taken Gandhi's advice to stand up and sustain themselves.

To be human in such a world is to resist institutionalized inhumanity, to confront the hypocrisy of the Rich World, to give our lives for those in need, and to receive from them the gift of hope.

*   *   *

Back at the hotel, we had a New Year's Eve dinner followed by a lecture by Arun's son, Tushar Gandhi, who runs the Mahatma Gandhi Foundation.

"Gandhi dreamed of a classless society living in perfect harmony, with no untouchability or drugs, with gender equality, and in peace with all the world," Tushar began. "This dream has not been fulfilled."

Tushar continued, "There is total disparity between rural poverty and urban wealth because India chose to seek industry, and so the urban areas exploded, leaving the rural villages in destitution. Many starve. Some farmers commit suicide because they cannot pay their interest. The rural areas are content with one day of electricity each week. Gandhi urged India to return to the spinning wheel because that would guarantee at least one meal a day to the starving masses. The government promotes technology and computers, but does nothing for the starving tribal peoples. So there are two Indias — the affluent, Westernized urban area versus the poor, rural areas. The politicians are corrupt, and the economy is at the mercy of the United States.

"Meanwhile, the villages are segregated by caste, which is why Gandhi fought so hard to abolish untouchability, to get rid of vertical castes and leave a horizontal caste system, so that all castes are equal and there is no exploitation. Gandhi dreamed of an India without classes or castes, but people are still killed because of their castes.

"Gandhi dreamed of equality between women and men, and though India has had a woman president, female fetuses are often aborted so that boys will be born. In some villages the birth rate is five to one for boys. Girls are deprived of education, told to stay at home, and require money for a dowry, so sexism thrives and kills in India.

"Finally, instead of becoming a peaceful nation, as Gandhi dreamed, India has rejected nonviolence and built nuclear weapons. India's military budget increased 35 percent this year. The government no longer even uses the word *nonviolence*. India as well as Pakistan have been decimated by weapons sales and the threat of war.

"Gandhi did not fail," Tushar concluded. "He proved that these points were achievable, but as a people, we have failed. The corporations have made India much worse. Nonetheless, India should take up Gandhi's dream. Many people are working hard to create new economic alternatives and promote equality."

Gandhi taught, "Materialism and morality have an inverse proportionality. The more materialistic we are, the more immoral we are." We have to reject materialism and strive for Gandhi's dream of a more just, peaceful, moral society.

Saturday, 1 January 2005

There is no comparing the Rich World of the United States with the poverty, starvation, homelessness, and sewage of India. So I will not compare them. Instead, I begin the New Year open to the blessings of India, to seeing India through Gandhi's eyes and welcoming its many gifts and traditions. Everywhere I go now, I greet people by putting my hands together in a prayer gesture and saying, "Namaste!" which means "The God of love within me greets the God of love within you." Beautiful!

The New Year began at five A.M. when we set off to the airport and flew off over Mumbai on a short flight to Poona. The view of Mumbai was shocking: an endless sea of tin roofs marking the shacks where millions survive urban poverty. Then, just as quickly, green fields, mesas, mountains, and barren desert lands appeared below. We arrived in Poona and set off for an all-day bus ride to Sangli. We saw rural India, with the masses lining the broken road, the sacred cows walking into the traffic, the green fields and yellow mustard flowers.

We arrived in Sangli at 8:30 that night, too late to visit a school project for slum children, but the children were there to greet us. Two girls put marigold garlands around my neck, and another painted the red dot, the *kumkum* mark, on my forehead (the first time in my life I had experienced that) to remind me of God, the duty of prayer, and the purpose of life. Then we drove to an auditorium for a session with area teachers, principals, and politicians. They spoke about their school projects and honored Arun by pledging to carry on Gandhi's vision of education for the poor. I was interviewed by a local journalist and met a young Indian priest, Father Paul, who runs twelve social centers and a huge parish with twelve thousand active parishioners. I also spoke with an elderly man dressed in full white khadi who told me about his time in prison and the day he met Gandhi when he was a teenager.

Sunday, 2 January 2005

Yesterday, rumors of another tsunami led to panic along the coastlines. We set off for another day in the countryside to visit Gandhian development programs founded by an extraordinary man, Arun Chavan, a former English professor who gave up his university career to implement Gandhi's vision and create social programs that would help the poor lift themselves out of poverty. He started the Verala Development Society, a community development program that models and advocates natural farming, education, housing, food distribution, and Gandhian societies that teach nonviolence and self-sufficiency.

We were brought to a beautiful farm, and we gathered in a circle of chairs in a cool grove of trees to hear the farmers describe their natural farming experiments — how they can take a quarter of an acre of the worst land and transform it in three years into rich, sustainable land that can feed five people. "The earth can sustain our needs, but not our greed," they quoted Gandhi as saying. "Gandhi taught us that the earth can sustain us, so we do not need outside help from the government or any other nation. It won't be coming anyway, so we turn to the earth. When we understand our connectedness with nature and work together with nature instead of exploiting it, we can live freely. But that means we must renounce greed."

I felt a marvelous peace sitting under these trees, listening to these heroic Gandhians taking responsibility for their lives and their impoverished neighbors. This whole region has suffered a drought in recent years, and many people have starved as a consequence. But those who remain have two hundred farmers working with them, creating self-sufficient farming communes.

At another rural cooperative, we heard how participants make bricks and help people build instant concrete houses. Over eighty million people are officially homeless in India. Here they make bricks and homes to house one another. They served us a beautiful lunch and sang for us as well. They were thrilled to have Arun with them.

Next we visited another village to watch a young theater troupe perform a short outdoor play that they perform in villages around the country. The musical portrays Lord Krishna returning to earth because he is worried about HIV/AIDS. With jokes and songs, the actors teach people about the disease and how to avoid it. Huge crowds of children and adults watched and laughed throughout the clever performance.

Then we were off to another village, to meet the local Gandhi society in a large auditorium. "We are all interrelated and interconnected," Arun told the crowd, "and we have to build relationships across the world, across the nations, to lessen the tensions and end the wars and injustice. Let us resolve today to work with every ounce of the strength we have for the rest of our lives for peace and a new, nonviolent world."

The sights and smells, the crowded streets, the speeding traffic, the cows and water buffaloes, the women carrying huge loads on their heads, the barefoot children. At the housing development compound, we were welcomed again with garlands of marigolds, jasmine, and roses. Throughout the day I was blessed by the people I met, and I pray for them all, all these beautiful, poor people, as well as for the tsunami victims, for India and the world, that we would help one another, empower one another, and create a new world full of justice and dignity for all.

*   *   *

In the afternoon we visited an alternative school built on a thousand acres for hundreds of students. During our first session we met some twenty "freedom fighters," men in their seventies and eighties who were part of the independence movement and who had known Gandhi. Sitting outside in a large square, surrounded by hundreds of young people, Arun Chavan, the founder, spoke to us about the need to work for a new, more human world, "not a world market, but a world community, a family of human beings. We don't have cultures," he said, "but vultures preying on humanity. Gandhi called us to live a natural life, not an artificial life. We want everyone to lead a happy life."

After his talk we were invited to plant trees on the school campus. A student gave me a banana plant and led me to a hole. Another showed us a boa constrictor and a cobra in a cage. One of the freedom fighters told me about meeting Gandhi in the early 1940s, and how he spent nine months in prison for nonviolent civil disobedience. I told him that I too had spent nine months in prison for civil disobedience against U.S. nuclear weapons. He could not believe it.

Finally we were taken to an outdoor park and stage on the campus for a performance by high-school students about the culture, songs, and dances of India. It was spectacular. It began with a six-year-old boy in full costume, banging on a drum to the rhythms of an old Indian song. A group of girls sang and danced to a tribal song; then one girl danced and lip-synched to a rock song. At the end a group of boys sang along to music. They were entertaining, funny, and inspiring. I was deeply moved, and after the poverty and pain I had witnessed, I felt hopeful for the first time, seeing not just the suffering and dying of the Indian people, but the rising, the hope and joy of India, beginning with its youth.

After dinner Arun spoke to us about Gandhi and his teachings. "Nonviolence is not just a strategy, but a way of life," he explained, quoting Gandhi's mandate. "Nonviolence resists not just physical violence and killings, but all forms of violence — economic violence, psychological violence, religious violence. And so it must be practiced on all fronts, from every angle, in order to create a new culture of nonviolence."

Monday, 3 January 2005

We had a long, scary drive back to Mumbai, weaving through the speeding jeeps, trucks, motorcycles, and the cows. Along the way we stopped at a weavers' cooperative and watched them make cloth, then had a meeting with the founder. Arun lit incense and put a garland on a beautiful portrait of his grandfather.

At four in the afternoon we drove through Poona to the former Aga Khan Palace, where Gandhi, his wife, Kasturbai, and a few other associates were imprisoned from 1942 to 1944. I remembered not only the scenes from the movie shot here, but the many letters Gandhi wrote from this place. We saw the rooms where they were imprisoned, their bathroom, their clothes, prison utensils, and shoes. It was here that Gandhi's secretary, Mahadev Desai, had a heart attack and dropped dead; a few months later, Kasturbai died in Gandhi's arms. Arun led us to the back to the garden, beyond a wall, to the place where Gandhi had cremated the two of them. I knelt down beside Arun to pray at Kasturbai's *samadhi*, the cremation place, and cried. I prayed too at the little white monument where a small portion of Gandhi's ashes are buried. Suddenly I was back before the graves of Martin Luther King, Dorothy Day, Philip Berrigan, Thomas Merton, Ita Ford, and Jean Donovan, praying for the world and for Gandhi's intercession, that I too might be an apostle of nonviolence.

We walked the gardens, sat outside, took pictures, and listened to Arun's explanation of their imprisonment. It was like visiting Robben Island, where Nelson Mandela was imprisoned, or Martin Luther King's jail cell, which I saw only last month at the Civil Rights Museum in Birmingham. I vividly recall sitting with Philip Berrigan in our cell, suffering through our confinement, but concluding that at least we were not going to die in jail. We were both deeply moved by the death of Kasturbai, who suffered the ultimate sacrifice of resistance, a perfect act of selfless love. I could not imagine getting seriously ill, much less dying, in prison.

I was standing on holy ground, charged with grace, suffering love, power, the cross, and the resurrection all in one. It was a mystical experience to walk the prison grounds where Gandhi walked, to step out on the balcony and to pass through the rooms where he lived for two years. The experience turned me back to the recent protest at the School of the Americas, and the possibility of crossing the line again someday and returning to prison.

Afterward we took the train from Poona to Mumbai and arrived at about ten P.M. at the old Victoria Station, where Gandhi was arrested in 1942. Outside, hundreds of beggars, hungry, homeless people, with missing arms and legs, greeted us as we caught the bus across Mumbai to the hotel.

Tuesday, 4 January 2005

It is immoral, even criminal, that the United States continues to spend over $100 billion to kill Iraqis, as well as countless other billions to build weapons, instead of healing the tsunami victims, abolishing hunger and disease, and eradicating poverty.

My friend Lynn Fredriksson sent an e-mail about the death of her friends in Ache, Indonesia, including a heroic woman who was a political prisoner, holed up in a crowded prison along the sea. The waves swept over the prison, and all were lost.

I pray that God will inspire us to heal and help the world's poor, especially these tsunami victims, that the Rich World will reject corporate greed, war, consumerism, and weapons, and focus on the urgent moral demand of our time: the elimination of poverty, hunger, disease, and war. I hope that, like Gandhi, we will heed the wisdom of nonviolence and become servants of peace, justice, and love.

Our group's first stop in crowded Mumbai was the laundromat. I would not have believed it had I not seen it with my own eyes. Mumbai is the only city in the whole world with a city-wide laundry system. Men collect your laundry, take it downtown to the public outdoor facility, scrub the clothes on open concrete slabs, hang them out to dry in the sun, and then later return them. No one can afford a washing machine, so everyone uses the facility. We stood on the street looking over the view of thousands of people scrubbing clothes.

Then we drove along Chowpatty Beach, where Gandhi led several political rallies and was arrested on several occasions, to the Prince of Wales Art Museum. I was stunned by the red-stone Buddhas and Boddhisattvas carved in the fifth century. They sat in perfect peace with half-smiles, inviting everyone to meditate and enter their peace. Upstairs I looked at the stone carvings from the Indus civilization that were made around 1000 B.C.E. But the Buddhas seemed to follow me around. Looking at them, I felt centered again, and I entered a new space, with new openings toward compassion. I felt disarmed and more peaceful. Could I learn to live and radiate such peace?

We spent the afternoon at Mani Bhavan, Gandhi's Mumbai house, two blocks from the ocean, where he lived and worked (when he wasn't traveling or living at the Sabarmati ashram) from 1917 to 1934. I spent a long time standing at the doorway to his second-story room, which has a balcony overlooking the street. The room has only a bare white mattress, a large white pillow, two spinning wheels, a writing stand, his walking stick, a pair of wooden sandals, a bookshelf, and a little statue of three monkeys saying, "Hear no evil, see no evil, speak no evil." The first floor has a library of Gandhi books, a photo exhibit, and a few artifacts, but the upstairs rooms and the balcony touched me deeply.

When Dr. King visited this place in 1958, he asked if he could spend the night alone in Gandhi's room. So they locked him in and left him alone, and when he emerged the next morning he said, "Now I have the moral courage to return to lead a movement for liberation."

In the meeting room we watched a documentary film on the 1930 Salt March, then discussed nonviolence with Arun. He told us about his meeting last August with Yasir Arafat in Palestine, his conversations with leading Palestinians about nonviolent resistance, and his invitation to Arafat to join him in a public demonstration against the new Israeli wall and the ongoing illegal Israeli occupation. Arafat declined to join the protest because he said he was afraid of being killed by the Israelis.

At night we drove past the famous "Gateway of India," where ships have entered India down through the centuries, and we boarded the ten P.M. overnight train to Ahmedabad. It was crowded and claustrophobic, but comfortable.

Wednesday, 5 January 2005

After breakfast at the hotel, we drove through Ahmedabad, across the Sabarmati River, to the Sabarmati ashram where Gandhi lived from 1917 to 1930. This ashram was the setting for all his major decisions in the freedom movement that led up to the Salt March of 1930.

We spent time first in the museum, looking at the photo exhibit, his letters, his prison journals, his sandals, walking sticks, watch, printing machines, and spinning wheels. Then I walked over to Gandhi's house, overlooking the river. It has a large veranda. His bare room connects to the open porch. It contains only a mattress, a one-foot-tall wooden desk, a bookshelf, and a large, dark spinning wheel. Kasturbai's room lies behind his, along with a small courtyard, kitchen, and guest room. I was so moved to be in his house. I walked around the grounds, went to the little hut next door where Vinoba Bhave lived in the early 1920s, followed by Mirabehn, the English woman who became Gandhi's assistant. On the other side of Gandhi's house is a marked-off, sandy prayer ground. Here the community met every morning and evening for prayers, silence, hymns, and Gandhi's reflections on nonviolence and the ashram vows. I walked around the guesthouse, where Nehru, Polak, Kollenbach, and others stayed, as well as the house of Gandhi's beloved nephew, Maganlal, who died suddenly in the late 1920s.

In 1989 some Gandhians gathered to create a new ashram community, so this sacred place would not just be a museum. Today, Manav Sadhna has seventy-nine people on staff and runs a variety of programs, including schools and soup kitchens throughout the nearby slums of Ahmedabad. Last week they walked into the slums and took up collections for the tsunami victims. People gave about fifteen cents each, 15 percent of their day's wage. We joined this group for their eleven A.M. prayer service, met the staff, and heard about their programs.

Then we drove across town to the new environmental sanitation center, built and directed by the ashram staff. The center, in a beautiful green park, has model alternative toilets and plumbing systems. Only 36 percent of India has access to adequate sanitation, making India one of the lowest nations for sanitation coverage. It has eight million dry latrines. Only 15 percent of the schools have toilets. Over four million children under the age of five die each year of diarrhea. Eighty percent of all diseases occur due to lack of sanitation and safe water.

After a delicious outdoor lunch, we waited for the dedication ceremony to begin. Finally the president of India arrived, Dr. A. P. J. Abdul Kalam. He was quite a character, in a gray suit with long gray hair parted down the middle. He took questions, made jokes, and basically refused to commit the Indian government to any serious sanitation funding and instead urged people to teach their children basic cleanliness skills.

*   *   *

Gandhi's Seven Deadly Sins (with an eighth, added by Arun):

Wealth without work
Pleasure without conscience
Knowledge without character
Commerce without morality
Science without humanity
Religion without sacrifice
Politics without principles
Rights without responsibilities

Thursday, 6 January 2005

A beautiful day, with a cool breeze and blue skies. It gets cold at night, but hot by noon. The headlines announce that the tsunami death toll has risen to 155,000. Nearly all of Ache province in Indonesia is gone. In Sri Lanka, fifty-nine Buddhist monks were sitting in the lotus position in their temple by the beach when the forty-foot-tall wave struck. Nine survived, but the rest were carried out to sea. They were pondering the impermanence of life; then they experienced it.

We drove back to the ashram and spent the morning visiting several of their cooperative projects, first their paper, soap, and yarn factories. I tried to use a spinning wheel much like Gandhi's, but the string kept breaking. It is more difficult than it looks. Arun showed us how to do it. He was taught by Gandhi himself, who later wrote Arun's parents that Arun had become faster than Gandhi. These projects apply Gandhi's dream of appropriate village technology to empower rural villagers to support themselves.

*   *   *

I'm sitting alone under a tree on an old stone bench, looking out over the river at the "Beautiful House" on the ashram grounds, where Nehru and Abdul Gaffer Kahn stayed, just across from Gandhi's house. The trees are full of noisy birds — black crows and green parrots. I'm soaking up the vibes of this holy ground, where they lived, loved, prayed, and organized revolutionary nonviolence. Across is the steel bridge where the crowds heard Gandhi speak the night before he left from here on the Salt March to Dandi, seventy-five years ago this April. The "Beautiful House" is boarded up now, but at the time, the guests loved the view.

God of peace, thank you for the grace, light, and peace that radiates from this holy ground, from Gandhi and these holy men and women. Inspire me to carry on their work of peace, love, service, and nonviolence, that I too may be a satyagrahi, *that I too may "love all and serve all," as their motto proclaims, that I too may be an apostle of nonviolence to our world of total violence, that I too may seek you through a life of service, prayer, community, solidarity, and organized nonviolence. May the whole world adopt the wisdom and way of nonviolence and receive your gift of peace. Amen.*

*   *   *

We drove through the slums, where 150,000 people suffer in shacks and sewage. Right in the middle we came upon an oasis, a free school for children run by the ashram. Dozens of widows volunteer, cooking, cleaning, and teaching. Thousands of children are served. The twenty-two-year-old director came from these streets at age twelve. They make sure the children get one good meal a day. The abject poverty is depressing, shocking, and upsetting, but their work is inspiring. When I was walking back to our truck through the alleyway, a little girl came running toward me, right through the sewage in the center of the alley. She was flying a ragged kite, about ten feet in the air, and she had a big, bright smile on her face. She whizzed past me, and I couldn't help but smile too. A glimpse of resurrection, even in the midst of this crucifixion.

Back at the ashram, we sat cross-legged on the floor and were presented with circular metal trays and served a variety of delicious, classic Indian dishes. It was the best food yet — spicy, home-cooked vegetarian Indian food.

Later we visited the SEWA Bank, a project of a credit union begun long ago by Gandhi to help poor women save money, get food, and improve their lives. The bank now has 34,000 women members, most of whom are illiterate. We then went to the SEWA headquarters to meet with the director, who told us, "The status of women in India continues to remain low. Eighty percent of all Indian women are rural, poor, illiterate, and unemployed. They have no jobs, stay at home in poverty, cannot read, and suffer under patriarchy and sexism. The goal of SEWA is the empowerment of women, which means economic development — money and food. We try to organize women. We have over ninety women's cooperatives, such as quilt-makers. They follow Gandhi's values. They pray every day, wear homespun khadi, and practice personal nonviolence toward all those they meet."

This evening Arun told us his life story, about growing up on the Phoenix Settlement ashram founded by his grandfather near Durban, South Africa, and coming to India to live with Gandhi at the age of twelve.

Friday, 7 January 2005

My friends Janet Chisholm and Judith Kelly and I skipped the long drive to the countryside to visit the rural SEWA project, and instead went back to the Gandhi ashram for a quiet day of retreat before tonight's nineteen-hour train ride to Delhi.

*   *   *

I'm sitting alone on the porch of Gandhi's house, meditating in the deep peace of this holy place. The tourists remove their shoes before stepping onto the stone slabs of the porch and exploring the bare rooms.

"Even a single lamp dispels the deepest darkness," Gandhi once said. I look out at the river, the green parrots and crows. The breeze blows through the trees, and I take a deep breath and all at once feel a deep peace. It is the dream of a lifetime to be here, a great blessing, like my retreat at Thomas Merton's hermitage. I recall Dr. King's need to spend the night in Gandhi's room in Mumbai, and reflect that I too need time in Gandhi's ashram house for strength to carry on the struggle for justice and peace. Here Gandhi lived and prayed and wrote and fasted and ate and slept. Here he planned the Salt March. From here he left on the great walk, expecting to be killed at any moment, or at least imprisoned for life. Here he let his light shine and dispelled the darkness of violence.

I pray that, like Elisha after the death of Elijah, I may receive a double portion of Gandhi's spirit. I pray for his mantle, to carry on his mission of active nonviolence. I know it is an absurd prayer, presumptuous and arrogant — who am I to ask such a thing? — but nonetheless, I want to carry on his work. Like Dr. King, I ask for the grace to fulfill the mission given to me to teach, promote, and practice Gospel nonviolence, to do my part for the struggle for justice and disarmament.

"Up here is seen the New Testament," Thomas Merton wrote from his porch. "That is to say, the wind comes through the trees and you breathe it." Here I breathe in the fresh air of peace. I feel healed, blessed, disarmed, reconciled, and sent forth again on the mission of transforming nonviolence.

Right at this moment, there are no other tourists. It is silent. I look around and take in this holy place. I recall my own journey, especially the endless hours spent discussing Gandhi's life, community, public work, and teachings with my friends in the Jesuit novitiate twenty-three years ago.

I send forth a prayer for peace upon the whole world, for a new spirit of nonviolence upon the human race, for a renewed dedication to humanity, a new commitment to compassion and liberation for the poor and disenfranchised.

Being here washes away my doubts, fears, anxieties, worries, resentments, and questions. All at once I feel restored, made whole. This is the culmination of a pilgrimage of twenty-five years and nine thousand miles. I can now head back to my hermitage in the desert and take up the campaign for nuclear disarmament, the closing of Los Alamos, the end of the Iraq war and the oppression of Palestinians, and the neglect of the world's sick and starving. I recall a letter in the museum that Gandhi wrote from here in 1922. In it he says he hopes to be arrested, to go to jail and gain "more triumphs of love." May we pursue those same goals and come to see our suffering, persecution, and arrests for justice and peace as "triumphs of love."

On a stone plaque by the door is the prayer of Gandhi: "Lord of humility, dwelling in the little hut. Help us to search for Thee throughout that fair land watered by Ganges, Brahmaputra, and Jamuna. Give us receptiveness. Give us openheartedness. Give us Thy humility. Give us the ability and willingness to identify ourselves with the masses of India. O God, who does help only when we feel utterly humble, grant that we may not be isolated from the people. We would serve as servants and friends. Let us be embodiments of self-sacrifice, embodiments of Godliness, humility personified, that we may know the land better and love it more."

Judith and Janet join me here on Gandhi's porch for quiet meditation. This moment of deep peace is the heart of my pilgrimage. I feel I have touched the soul of India, and I am blessed for my return to the American empire.

*   *   *

We stayed for several hours, reflecting on the trip, discussing what we had seen, sharing insights about Gandhi's life, and dreaming about what lay ahead in our own lives. Later, back at the hotel, our friends told us about their trip to the farming commune, and then we headed out to the over-night train to Delhi.

Gandhi's house and ashram life stand in sharp contrast to the lives of North American power-brokers, especially the great hypocrites Bush, Cheney, Rumsfeld, Powell, and Ashcroft. In Gandhi we see real leadership, real vision, someone who understands true peace, who cares for all peo-ple, not just the rich, who intends to serve the whole human race, not just his "base." This visionary leadership is completely missing in the United States. Our so-called leaders are really misleaders. They are blind, im-moral, greedy, and insane with power and violence, leading the massacre of Iraqis and the ongoing development of the world's largest stockpile of weapons of mass destruction. Gandhi, on the other hand, offers the exam-ple of a peaceful visionary who models the life of peace and shows us the path toward a future of peace.

Saturday, 8 January 2005

We have to keep working to disarm the world, even though it seems an im-possible task. We do not know the results of our actions, as Gandhi pointed out; they are in God's hands. But we have to keep working for jus-tice and peace. We have to do what we can to make a difference, to be part of the global movements for nonviolent change.

We arrived in the crowded Delhi train station after a long night on the train, then set off for the Birla Mansion, where Gandhi spent the last four months of his life, and where he was killed as he walked to his evening prayer service on January 30, 1948. The house is a massive white building where the millionaire industrialist G. D. Birla lived. It contains a mu-seum, photo exhibit, bookstore, and gift shop, surrounded by beautiful gardens.

On the front right side of the house, near the street, is a little wing where Gandhi stayed. In his room are some of his possessions — small ta-bles, mattresses, spinning wheels, sandals, walking sticks, a knife, a paper-weight, and his glasses. On the porch sits the cot where he fasted to the point of death in January 1948 to stop the Delhi riots. Here over fifty Hindu and Muslim leaders pledged to stop the killing. Gandhi's kidneys had shut down, but still he said their pledge would not be enough. Then he burst into tears. But they begged him to live, promising they would never support riots or violence again. So he broke his fast. The next day, January 20, 1948, a bomb went off during his prayer meeting.

Earlier, Arun told us that he thought the Indian government did nothing to protect Gandhi after he was nearly killed by that bomb. He believes they concluded that a dead, martyred Gandhi was better than a live, trouble-making Gandhi. Years after Gandhi's death, Arun and his mother met twice with the brother of Gandhi's assassin (who was executed) to learn why Gandhi had been killed. Though the two had forgiven him, they broke off the dialogue with his brother when they realized that he still supported the assassination.

Through the door of this room Gandhi walked to his death. The path now has raised concrete steps to mark that final journey. The backyard is a magnificent lawn and garden. Gandhi held interfaith prayer services here every evening at five. He sat on a raised platform against the far back wall, next to the servants' quarters, so that everyone could see him. As he approached his seat, he was shot. A stone monument marks the place where he was killed.

We were brought to a large, covered auditorium for a prayer service of Hindu hymns that Gandhi loved. The elderly woman who led us had performed here for Gandhi when she was a teenager. She played a harmonium, while others played the bongos and a sitar. The opening instrumental music was the most heavenly, spiritual music I have ever heard. It moved me to tears. The woman concluded with Gandhi's favorite hymn, *Vaishnava Jana:*

> *One who is truly virtuous feels others' sufferings as his own. He serves others in distress, and lets no conceit enter his mind. He honors everyone in the world and speaks ill of no one ever. He preserves purity in thought, word, and deed. He treats all alike. He has renounced all craving. Never does his tongue utter untruth. Never does he covet another's wealth. He is freed of attachment and delusion and is abiding in renunciation. Ever devoted to the holy name of God, all places of pilgrimage he finds within himself. He is devoid of all greed and cunning. He has abdicated passion and anger. To revere such a one will bring salvation for generations to come.*

Afterwards I visited with the director of the museum, who told me about the large youth conferences she conducts to teach young Indians about Gandhi's nonviolence. But then, with great emotion, she asked me to do what I could to help stop U.S. global domination and wars. "The U.S. is the greatest source of violence in the world today," she said, "and you all need to be converted to nonviolence more than anybody else."

*   *   *

"Just as the art of violence lies in killing," Gandhi once said, "the art of nonviolence lies in dying, without a trace of violent retaliation." I walk slowly, mindfully across the lawn up to the place where he was killed. All at once I am transported back to Memphis to the Lorraine Motel balcony where I had gone to pray over Dr. King's martyrdom; to the chapel in San Salvador where Archbishop Romero was killed while saying mass; to the remote field where four U.S. churchwomen were raped and killed on December 2, 1980; to the church in the old city of Jerusalem marking the crucifixion of Jesus. This beautiful, sad, mysterious place invites me into the mystery of the cross, to that sacrificial, suffering, redemptive love which dies and offers itself for humanity rather than dominate or kill others, and I am summoned again to walk the path as Gandhi did, literally a path of peace to the prayer garden to meet the assassin's bullet and face death. I pray to bear the same spirit of love and sacrifice that Gandhi bore as he walked the path of nonviolence to martyrdom, that I too might share the love and gift of Jesus as he goes to the cross and the new life of resurrection.

Sunday, 9 January 2005

We're back on the morning train to Dehradun, with sitar and drum music playing overhead as India's countryside passes by. Green fields, palm trees, blue sky — but also barren desert, garbage piles, children in rags, thousands of people, dilapidated two-story buildings, stray dogs, sacred cows, water buffaloes, goats, dirt paths, sewage, and auto rickshaws.

Watching India pass by, I hear Jesus call me once again to renounce my selfishness and become like him, the servant of all and the least of all, to give my life in nonviolent, suffering love for humanity, to be a missionary of nonviolence and an apostle of peace. I say "Yes" with all my heart and beg for these graces, for his cross and creative nonviolence, that my life might bear good fruit and shine a bright light to dispel the utter darkness of these terrible times. Amen.

After lunch at the hotel, we were privileged to spend the afternoon with one of the world's leading antiglobalization and environmental activists, Dr. Vandana Shiva, a brilliant, engaging scientist and Gandhian activist. "Gandhi's legacy is a legacy of love, compassion, and sacrifice," she began. "In the 1970s, in response to deforestation, women in the women's movement started hugging the trees, saying, 'You will have to kill us before you cut the trees.' In 1981 we had a terrible flood, and a four-mile lake was formed because of deforestation, and after that, finally, the women were listened to."

She continued, "Gandhi's Salt March was so imaginative, so inspirational. Unjust laws are meant to be disobeyed, to create a moral order. Dr. King and Mandela used that same philosophy. Gandhi shifted the mind of the world. Environmentalists started to do with forests what Gandhi did with salt. A huge forest *satyagraha* campaign was started. Thirty-nine people were killed, but there are forest *satyagrahas* around the world now. Why? Unjust laws are not meant to be obeyed. We must have the courage to break them nonviolently to protect humanity and the earth.

"When the new world order called 'globalization' was laid out, they wanted to create a monopoly on seeds, control all the farms, and claim patents for every seed. Five companies would control all the food in the world, and so all health. Gandhi opposed England with the spinning wheel by getting people to make their own clothes. So we grow every crop, save all the seeds, and build model farming villages so that we can take care of our own lives. *Satyagraha* is the courage to noncooperate with injustice. *Swadhesi* means making your own things through your own hard work. *Swaraj* is the ability to govern yourself, not just on the state level but at every level — personal, communal, regional, and international. Instead of a pyramid, with the top crushing the bottom, Gandhi envisioned oceanic circles where every person is the center of the world, where everyone relates with respect and dignity to everyone else. So we support *satyagraha*, *swadhesi*, and *swaraj*.

"Free trade is meant only for a handful of businesses," she said. "Wal-Mart requires the disappearance of all small shops. This so-called free trade will lead to the total control of society, nature, economics, and politics, a new economic totalitarianism. Today we no longer have a state; we have a corporate state. All decisions regarding agriculture around the world are now run by the World Trade Organization. Globalization has reduced all agriculture to three crops — soy, corn, and potatoes — which creates disease. A billion people go hungry. Another billion get sick from these wrong foods. This crazy system leads to poverty. Gandhi urged us to work with the earth to produce for ourselves what we need and to noncooperate with these injustices.

"The WTO is wrecking the world's agriculture," she continued. "We have no farming communes. By 2004, sixteen thousand farmers had committed suicide in India because of debts. The violence of chemicals used on the earth are the new weapons of mass destruction. So this is war, and we are a peace movement, protecting the species and farmers and all people. We don't call people 'consumers.' Anyone who eats participates in the food chain. We have to be conscious about food and choose what to eat. So we have started three Gandhian movements. First, we have started a campaign to not pay the unjust tariffs for water. When we announced this campaign, the government postponed the collection. Now we will protest the diversion of the rivers to Delhi, so that this water will remain for the villages. We work village to village, creating units of 'water democracy.' We are fighting privatization and river diversion.

"Second, we disobey these new patent laws claiming ownership of all seeds. Gandhi collected salt. We grow indigenous seeds and collect them and save them, which is a crime. We violate the patent laws. A higher moral duty calls us to break these laws. We are starting seed banks and co-operate with the higher law which says that seeds belong to all six billion people, not six companies.

"Third, we protest Coke, which uses toxic chemicals to wash bottles and leaves the chemicals in the groundwater. So we targeted the Coke plant in Kerela. They shut down the plant. Some eighty-seven other Coke plants pollute the water. We are trying to protect our water, and we have more protests coming up. These movements carry on Gandhian philosophy. Women have started these movements because the men are off washing dishes in Delhi. The environmental movement is more robust here in the Third World because the issues are so deadly. These are terrible but exciting times, and we do our best.

"The tsunami was a dress rehearsal for the disasters that are coming. The ice caps are melting. There will be no more Maldive Islands or coastal areas in a few decades. This is where we are headed. Around the world, people are taking Gandhian actions. These actions will never end. There's always something we can do. But we have to take responsibility."

The institute that Dr. Shiva heads offers courses and farming programs, conferences and lectures; it trains farmers and students and organizes campaigns for justice. After her extraordinary presentation, Bob Daniels and I went for a long walk through Dehradun to mull over her inspiring words and example. She is the greatest Gandhian we have met so far.

Monday, 10 January 2005

This morning we drove north into "the foothills of the Himalayas" to visit Navdanya Farm, Dr. Shiva's farming commune ten miles north of Dehradun, and Bija Vidyapeeth, a college for sustainable living and global alternatives where students learn cooking, gardening, composting, farming, yoga, and anti-globalization organizing. Navdanya Farm grows over six hundred plants, with 250 types of rice, and preserves the seeds.

They speak here of Gandhi's vision of oceans of love — personally, communally, nationally, and globally. If you spend your life in selfless service to the poor and do good works, an ocean of love will grow inside you. Just as you can't set an ocean on fire, so too nothing will be able to disturb you because you have an interior ocean of love. When we organize communities of love around the world, we transform the world with tsunamis of nonviolence and truth and disarming love.

We visited the seed banks, dark rooms with walls of tin cans filled with every indigenous seed around. They are saving and reproducing the seeds, and are trying to create seed banks across the country. We also spent hours walking through the beautiful farm fields.

I was reminded of the Beatitude from the Sermon on the Mount:

"Blessed are the meek, for they shall inherit the earth." Here, the meek, the gentle, the nonviolent are saving the earth and inheriting the earth. Indeed, they are greatly blessed.

*   *   *

"The purpose of nonviolence is to create a culture of nonviolence," Arun told us during our afternoon discussion. "We have to begin to build non-violent relationships, to create a nonviolent society where conflicts are reduced, and to create nonviolent institutions. We need to simplify our lives, share our resources with the poor, and eliminate injustice."

"It's time to take extreme nonviolent measures," the editorial in the *Hindustan Times* stated today. "We have to keep reminding ourselves that the U.S. administration and people like Osama bin Laden actually need love each other and feed off each other. In this sense, bin Laden's archaic but simply delivered Arabic oratory outlining a shining 'Islamic' utopia and George Bush's crude pronouncements proclaiming his desire to bring 'freedocracy' to all corners of the world are two sides of the same coin. They are thinly disguised posturings for what actually turn both men on: the fantasy of absolute power, the love of spectacular violence, and the free-flowing blood of innocents. Both sides love and preach violence. In this, their joint framing of the planet, the wreckage caused by the big waves is but a small blip in the larger story. Expect their fanatical tsunami to piggy-back on the geological one — and then try and figure out ways to get out of its path. Because though it may have receded into the background for the moment, their tsunami of violence is actually and potentially far more devastating than the churning unleashed by the tectonic plates below the Indian Ocean."

Tuesday, 11 January 2005

We were up at three A.M. to catch the train back to Delhi, where we went first to Rajghat, the park that holds Gandhi's cremation place. It's a long walk through green lawns and flowers. You remove your shoes and enter the large courtyard and walk in silence to the center, where there is a long black concrete slab, two feet off the ground, about ten yards by ten yards. An eternal flame is lit on one side. Tourists crowd around it. Some kneel. Others touch it. No one says a word.

Arun walks up and kneels down in prayer. I kneel beside him. I look up at the blue sky and lift a prayer for peace, for the poor, for India, for the whole world.

"Nonviolence is not a garment to be put on and off at will," Gandhi once said. "Its seat is in the heart, and it must be an inseparable part of our very being. There is no such thing as defeat in nonviolence. It shall be proved by persons living it in their lives with utter disregard of consequences to themselves. One person who can express nonviolence in life exercises a force superior to all the forces of brutality."

Later in the afternoon we toured Qutab Minar, the ancient historic Hindu-Muslim ruins, temples, and mosques in a large park that dates back over a thousand years. In the center stands a five-story tower. After centuries of violence at the hands of the Hindus, the Muslims tore down the Hindu temples and used their stones to build these mosques. They are astonishingly beautiful and horrific at the same time. The history of Hindu-Muslim faith and violence is embodied in this one place.

Later we drove through Delhi, past the Gate, the Vice Royal Palace, the parade grounds, and through the wide streets. We watched a dance troupe perform a variety of Indian dances for us, then enjoyed a farewell dinner. Sherrill Hogen from Massachusetts read her poem entitled "A Letter," about Gandhi's dream of a peace army, "Shanti Sena":

Gandhiji,

This world of violence
took you down,
your message too strong
too true
for it to bear.
This world of violence
makes mothers cry out
makes even fathers weep.

74

But we are building
your Shanti Sena
one project at a time.
We are learning courage
where fear and fire rule.
We are marching under one heaven
carrying basketsful of food
buckets of clean water.
We are planting seeds and trees
saving whales
and playing with the children

because neither hate nor greed
nor death
can take you from us.

Wednesday, 12 January 2005

"The debate about the 'stinginess of the American government' should not be restricted to the ongoing tsunami relief operations," *The Times of India* said in an editorial today. "The U.S agenda outlines increased defense spending, the need to challenge regimes hostile to American interests, and the necessity of having an international order friendly to U.S. interests. Such an agenda is reflected in the initial tardy response to the disaster and also in U.S. assistance to developing nations. According to estimates, the U.S. gives only 15 cents for every $100 of national income, which makes it rank last among the top 22 donor countries. The priorities of the U.S. become clear when one contrasts the aid for tsunami relief with the amount spent on Iraq.

"The $350 million pledged for victims of the tsunami is loose change when compared to the $148 billion spent on Iraq. In fact the entire U.S. budget for assistance to developing nations works out to less than one-ninth of the cost of the war in Iraq. It can be justifiably argued that the neo-conservative agenda of attacking unfriendly regimes with the dubious aim of spreading 'freedom' undercuts American assistance for disaster relief as well as development projects in poor countries. Unless American foreign policy can break free from the neo-conservative straitjacket, this disparity between the money spent on aid and war will remain."

* * *

We took the train to Agra and spent the morning visiting the ancient Agra Fort, built in the late 1500s by Emperor Akbar, with its huge red-brick walls, colonnaded arches, and courtyards. The roofs were covered with green parrots and brown monkeys.

After lunch we drove out to the countryside, past large brown walls and structures, onto the grounds of the Taj Mahal. We were overwhelmed by the white marble monument with its beautiful pools and gardens. As you walk toward it, it appears to change, and becomes even more beautiful. It does not seem real — it seems more like a living postcard. It is an astonishing work of art.

Afterwards we had a six-hour drive back to Delhi. We passed miles of mustard fields, green grass with bright yellow flowers on top, as well as white birch trees and crowds of people. A big red sun took its time setting in the distance. The beauty and heartbreak and magic and tragedy and gift and horror and joy and injustice and grace of India seemed to surround me. Ultimately it is a land of love and peace because these poor people are people of love and peace, and I am blessed to be here.

Thursday, 13 January 2005

As the tsunami death toll approaches 230,000, I know there is another tsunami of violence, injustice, and corporate greed that crushes the world's poor, leaving forty thousand people dead from hunger each day, and how many countless more sick from war or relievable disease. One hundred fifty thousand children die every month from malaria in Africa alone.

Though the terrible acts of the U.S. government upon the world's poor depress me, I feel inspired with new hope, strength, and energy by the people I have met in India who organize grassroots projects to empower the poor and resist injustice. They are living out Gandhi's vision in the face of overwhelming obstacles. I cannot let myself off the hook. They challenge me to do likewise, to be part of a global grassroots movement for justice and peace that will one day in the future transform the world.

"On the whole, in India, the prognosis is — to put it mildly — Not Good," Arundhati Roy writes in one of her essays. "And yet, one cannot help but marvel at the fantastic range and depth and wisdom of the hundreds of people's resistance movements all over the country. They're being beaten down, but they simply refuse to lie down and die. . . . What we need to search for and find, what we need to hone and perfect into a magnificent, shining thing, is a new kind of politics, not the politics of governance, but the politics of resistance, the politics of opposition, the politics of forcing accountability, the politics of joining hands across the world and preventing certain destruction. In the present circumstances, I'd say that the only thing worth globalizing is dissent. It's India's best export."

* * *

"Christ died on the cross with a crown of thorns on his head, defying the might of a whole empire," Gandhi wrote. "And if I raise resistance of a nonviolent character, I simply and humbly follow in the footsteps of the great teachers."

Janet, Judith, and I spent the morning at the Gandhi National Museum in Delhi. We took our time walking through the huge photo exhibit and studying his personal effects, such as his copy of Ruskin's book *Unto This Last* and Tolstoy's *The Kingdom of God Is Within You*, the walking stick he used on the Salt March, his spoons, forks, false teeth, microscope, law books, clothes, and yarn, and all the possessions from his last day, including the bedsheets, blankets, and the blood-stained clothes he was wearing when he was killed. I was deeply moved by these relics, and prayed that I too might give my life for justice, peace, and the world's nonviolent transformation.

Later we walked back to Rajghat. Now I sit alone here on the top stone veranda, looking down on the courtyard where the black stone cremation memorial is surrounded by crowds of tourists. I feel a cool breeze and watch hundreds of Indians pass by in silence. I look up at the blue sky and give thanks: *Dear God, thank you for this pilgrimage to Gandhi's India. Send me back now to the American empire as a pilgrim of peace, that I too may be an instrument of your peace, that I too may walk the way of nonviolence, that I too may shine the light of peace in a world of war, that I too may be a force of truth and love in a world of lies and fear, that my life too might bear the good fruit of peace and justice like Gandhi's, that I too may be a disciple of Jesus and a servant of peace, in Jesus' name. Amen.*

Friday, 14 January 2005

The flight from Delhi to Mumbai was delayed last night. The waiting room in Delhi was filled with hundreds of bearded, elderly men wearing only white sheets. They periodically knelt down on the ground for prayers. They were on their way to Mecca for the annual Haj pilgrimage.

Because of the delay, I didn't get to my room until midnight. Then I was up at three for the six A.M. flight to Paris. We had a long layover there, then a long flight to Newark, New Jersey, where I arrived around five P.M. An exhausting day. My head is full of India and prayers and hopes and expectations for my return to New Mexico on Sunday.

Saturday, 15 January 2005

After a good night's sleep, I joined Steve Kelly, S.J., for morning mass at the local parish for his birthday. Then we took the subway downtown with Daniel Berrigan for the peace vigil and march in honor of Dr. King's birthday. At noon we gathered with anti-war banners and signs at Times Square in front of the Armed Forces Recruiting Station. I handed out leaflets denouncing Bush's war on Iraq and invoking Dr. King's vision of nonviolence. Then we marched in single-file silence to the Hudson River and the *S.S. Intrepid*, the battleship turned into a war museum. Over twenty members of our group blocked the entrance and were arrested. Afterwards, Dan, Steve, and I spent a few relaxing hours enjoying soup and coffee at a nearby café and catching up with one another.

Tonight the West Side Jesuit Community threw a dinner party for

Steve's birthday, and I spoke about my trip. I stayed up late with Dan talking about the country, the work ahead, and our hopes and dreams. I'm glad to be back, eager to return to New Mexico, and grateful for this upbeat day of protest and friendship in honor of Dr. King. A good way to restart my life back in the American empire.

May my Indian pilgrimage and the example of Mahatma Gandhi and his suffering, faithful people push me further on the journey to justice, nonviolence, and peace.

CHAPTER 13

Witness for Peace in Colombia

Tuesday, 14 February 2006, Panama City, Panama

It's ninety degrees here, hot and humid, but beautiful. We flew in low under the clouds at sunset, along the Canal, from the Atlantic to the Pacific, and then around the beautiful city rising up from the ocean with its lush green mountains in the background and big ships coming and going. Panama has suffered war and occupation, but it remains beautiful.

A long day, from Albuquerque to Houston to Panama and on to Bogotá. I'm going to Colombia to meet two heroic Jesuits, prophets of justice and peace: Javier Giraldo and Pacho de Roux. Then to join a delegation of the Colombia Support Network in the countryside to learn about the war and what we can do to help stop it.

This pilgrimage was born ten years ago when a Colombian woman showed up at my door asking me to go with her to her country to learn about their hidden war and the U.S. involvement in it. Sure, I said, someday I'll go with you. In similar fashion, she tracked down Bishop Thomas Gumbleton, Father Roy Bourgeois, and even Noam Chomsky, and brought them all to Colombia as part of her project, the Colombia Support Network.

Cecilia Zarate-Laun and I became friends, and we stayed in touch. Last fall we toured Wisconsin together with Kathy Kelly, speaking to churches and college audiences about the reality of war and our work for peace. Now, finally, the time has come for me to go with my friend Cecilia to Colombia, to make that long pilgrimage for peace into the dark night of Colombia's hidden war.

Rich in natural resources, Colombia has over forty-five million people. And yet, three and a half million of them are internally displaced, the highest number in the Western hemisphere — even though Colombia is not at war with another nation. Thirty people are assassinated every single day in Colombia for political reasons, some ten thousand a year, nearly two hundred thousand over the last few decades, the highest homicide rate in the world. These killings come after a history of death. Between 1948 and 1960, another two hundred thousand were killed. It also has the highest number of kidnappings annually in the world. As one of the Jesuits would say, "Colombia is one of the most violent places on earth."

Colombia's government is technically a democracy, with an elected president — Alvaro Uribe — but actually it is more like a dictatorship. It has the façade of a democracy, but the reality is that a handful of corrupt politicians work for the brutal Colombian military, and tens of thousands of paramilitary troops roam the beautiful countryside — ostensibly in pursuit of the rebel groups (FARC and ELN) under the direction of the United States and its military advisors — to rid it of its indigenous peoples, steal their land, and give it to their multinational corporations so they can make massive profits in oil, gold, and other resources. Colombia is a complicated stew of violence, with the greatest human rights violations in the Western hemisphere, and the U.S. government is stirring the pot.

In particular, the Colombian government and army set up thousands of paramilitaries to do their dirty work. The United States suggested that the Colombian army set them up so that the army would not be criticized for human rights violations and U.S. military aid would not have to be cut. So the paramilitaries do most of the killings and the massacres, and the Colombian army looks the other way and then continues to receive millions from the Pentagon. The army trains the paramilitaries, hides them, and gives them lists of the names of people to be killed. The army protects the oil fields and the mining areas and the multinational corporations, while the paramilitaries enforce the overall repression of the poor. They are funded by the rich — the president, the industrialists, the landowners, cattlemen, drug lords, multinationals. But now they have become a power unto themselves, like the death squads of El Salvador.

I go to Colombia to stand with my sisters and brothers, to meet these great Jesuits, to learn about the struggle for life — and yes, to fulfill Jesus' commandment to love our enemies, to make peace. I go as a friend, a brother, and a servant, to offer a living sign of solidarity, love, friendship, and peace.

Bogotá, Colombia

At the crowded airport, the great man himself met me. Small, thin, balding, in a gray suit and sweater, sixty-one-year-old Javier Giraldo did not look like one of Latin America's towering giants of human rights with his shy, gentle smile. Actually, according to friends, he is the single greatest threat to the Colombian military. Between his broken English and my broken Spanish, we got on just fine. He took me to the Jesuit high school, Colegio San Bartolomé Merced, where Cecilia later met me. A great beginning, to be welcomed by two such heroes.

Wednesday, 15 February 2006

A few months ago, PBS News asked President Bush about the future of Iraq. "The future of Iraq is Colombia," he grinned. Iraq has been destroyed, its resources stolen, its people crushed, and its government taken over, as the whole world now knows. I think Bush is serious. He prefers his war in Colombia, where the United States wipes away the indigenous peoples, steals their land, gives it to its multinational corporations, and maintains a façade of democracy, all under the guise of the noble cause, the war against drugs — like Bush's charade in Iraq, his war against terrorism, his fight for freedom. The United States carries out the same killing spree in Colombia, but no one knows about it. Bush wants to control Iraq ultimately, just like the United States controls Colombia — without the rest of the world knowing about it. This is why I have come here — to enter the darkness of U.S. imperialism and shine a light of truth on its evil works.

Father Francisco "Pacho" de Roux

As in every war and injustice, good people emerge as heroes of peace and justice. Though Colombia's institutional church leaders by and large support the war against the poor, two Jesuits have stood up for years to advocate for human rights and peace. They have endured persecution, harassment, death threats, and exile, but they carry on the struggle for truth and justice.

This morning I had the great opportunity to visit with Jesuit Father Francisco de Roux, known as Pacho. He began by summing up the situation in Colombia: "President Uribe is a close friend of George W. Bush. He is the only Latin American president to support the U.S. war on Iraq. Like Bush, he thinks the solution to everything is war. Here, everyone — the government, the paramilitaries, the landowners, and the rebels — thinks the only solution is war.

"The rebel groups — the FARC and the ELN rebels — fight the Colombian state. We, on the other hand, try to transform the laws and institutions. We all agree that we need profound structural change in Colombia, but some of us do not think war or terrorism will bring peace.

"We are trying to help the people to participate in the reconstruction of their country. All the regions of Colombia are different. The only way we can rebuild our broken country is through its people. I am starting in Magdalena Medio, the region along the river between Bogotá and the Caribbean, with our program 'Development and Peace.' The European Union has funded us for eight years.

"We are not waiting for several decades for the peace process to begin. We are starting now to transform ourselves. We have started peace conversations, negotiations, and agricultural programs. We speak with the guerrillas, the paramilitaries, the soldiers, and the multinationals — hoping to bring peace. We try to recover our human dignity, reclaim our rights, and create a new world where everyone is treated like the president and the pope.

"The landowners expel the peasants, produce displaced people by the millions, through their paramilitaries. We are promoting disarmament. Our development work is a means to create human dignity and human rights. The project reveals the structural injustice we suffer. We expose it and work to solve it.

"We have never accepted Plan Colombia. If you work with it, you are part of the conflict. You end up taking sides, against the guerrillas, and that will never bring peace. When I have problems with the guerrillas or the soldiers or get death threats from paramilitary groups, people tell me to leave, but I stay and consider it an invitation to talk. I go and meet with them and try to build understanding.

"Twenty-three people in our project have been killed. Three years ago, paramilitaries killed a fantastic woman on our staff, the team coordinator for a rural area. We found her body. It had no arms, legs, or head. The message was 'Leave this area at once!' It was very hard for all of us. So I went to see the head of the paramilitaries, the man responsible for her death.

"'I presume you think that what you are doing is the best thing you can do for Colombia,' I said. 'Please understand that I'm trying to do the best I can for Colombia too, only without weapons or warfare. I do not agree with your behavior. You are generating enormous difficulties for our people.'

"'This was an act of war,' he said. 'She was a lawyer bringing charges against us, so we considered her an enemy, and we had to kill her.'

"On another occasion, the guerrillas held a tribunal against us, against me. They said, 'You are bringing capitalism to our region and telling people not to join us.' I thought for sure they would kill me, that I would be killed that very day. But I went to speak with them too, and after our conversation, they developed more confidence in us.

"None of us in Colombia, myself included, have the freedom to live independently from war. We all suffer from it — by what we do or don't do. So we try to help our people rebuild their region, and we work with everyone, all of us, poor people, guerrillas, soldiers, paramilitaries, government officials. It's an enormous project and very complicated. But we have to act and try to stop the violence.

"When we started our program, the region was first controlled by the guerrillas, then the paramilitaries. But now through our program, little by little, the people themselves are taking control of the area. The people are taking initiative. We started what we call 'humanitarian spaces,' areas where we try to protect life, promote dignity, distribute land, and force the government to assume responsibility. We are teaching them nonviolence. There is new determination and confidence among the people, even in the face of death threats. Over the years, both the guerrillas and the paramilitaries are realizing that violence is not the way. You can help us by getting people in the United States to understand the relationship of their country to Colombia, especially your connection with the Colombian military."

CINEP, the Center for Investigation and Popular Education

Later in the morning, I visited with Jesuit Father Alejandro Angulo, director of CINEP, the Center for Investigation and Popular Education, an enormous social research center that publishes books, reports, and magazines on various aspects of Colombia. Sixty people staff the center, which is located in a five-story building next to the Jesuit high school. Several floors make up its widely used research library.

"This is a civil war, a class war," Father Angulo told me as we toured the center. "The FARC and the ELN both started with a desire for agrarian reform, which Colombia's president promised back in the 1950s. But those reforms were never passed into law, so people left the countryside and moved into the cities. The main objective of the war is land. The landowners formed the paramilitaries to steal the land from the people and claim it. Today the FARC continues to use an old model of land reform. The paramilitaries represent capitalism and economic and social exploitation. In recent years the paramilitaries have begun to fight themselves. They have become a wholly independent movement with some thirty thousand soldiers. They are well funded and present in every section of the country.

"The army is technically separate from the paramilitaries, but they cross over. There are some 120,000 soldiers in the Colombian army, but the government is trying to double it. There are twenty thousand rebels. Most of the daily assassinations are made to look like car crashes or robberies."

Father Angulo spoke about the Jesuits, how most of them go about their business working in schools and parishes, never speaking out or doing anything about the war. "In the 1980s, a Jesuit, Father Sergio Restrepo, a published poet, was working in a parish when the paramilitaries took over his area. He painted a mural inside his church and outside on the walls, with themes about justice and peace and freedom from slavery. Soon afterwards he was brutally killed. His body was left in front of the church.

"Francisco de Roux has received many death threats. Sometimes he has to go to Europe to get away, but now he has decided to stay. They could kill him, but he is too well-known. He speaks to the European Union each year, and occasionally to U.S. Senate committees.

"Javier Giraldo is the most well-known advocate for human rights in Colombia. He started his human-rights database almost thirty years ago. He has documented every killing in the country for decades. He has kept a complete record of the atrocities by the Colombian government and its forces, and has been critical of the rebels as well. He publishes an enormous quarterly periodical called *Noche Niebla [Night and Fog]*, deliberately using the Nazi name for its strategy of genocide. He registers every death. When he gets enough evidence, he takes generals to court, even though he's never had a verdict or a resolution in his favor. He has now even started to hold press conferences to denounce the massacres.

"Javier, too, has suffered countless death threats, and retreated to Europe and the United States on several occasions. From the beginning he was targeted by the government. He does not hide, but he is careful. He lives downtown at the Jesuit high school, next door to the presidential palace and the Congress building. Many of his friends have been killed, but he keeps at it. It's a miracle he has not been killed."

After speaking with Father Angulo, I met with Father Fernan Gonzalez, a Jesuit historian who has spent decades studying Colombia's dark history of violence. "First there was the genocide of the native peoples," he began. "Then in the last half of the eighteenth century, Spanish domination brought further violence to the region. As the population grew, the big landowners set up the paramilitary groups, and eventually guerrilla groups appeared in the rural areas. Now the FARC controls certain villages and rural areas, sometimes with the drug lords, while the government and its armies wage war throughout the country. The countryside is a disaster. We need to end the war, but we also need a new Marshall Plan to rebuild our land, transportation, villages, and cities."

The Fortieth-Anniversary Mass for Camilo Torres

That afternoon Javier Giraldo took me across town to the National University for a special mass being held in the university chapel to mark the anniversary — forty years ago today — of the killing of Camilo Torres, the priest and popular university chaplain who joined the rebels. Camilo

86

Torres worked here and even built the large concrete chapel where we celebrated mass. The church was packed with students and faculty. Just as Javier, myself, and several other priests processed to the altar, two dozen students, wearing red-and-black clothes, marched up the aisles and remained standing there for half of the mass. They were members of one of the rebel groups, and they were trying to honor Camilo Torres. (Personally I wish they had stayed for the whole mass and honored Camilo by adhering to Jesus and his way of nonviolent resistance. But I was there to listen and pray.)

Javier preached eloquently about Camilo, how he gave his life for justice and peace, how he longed to reconcile all the people of Colombia with one another, how he hoped one day that the war would end and he would return to his pastoral work. Everyone applauded. Then two of the revolutionaries took the pulpit and started shouting about Camilo and the struggle for justice. One of them ended by chanting, "The country or death!" (Again, I thought Father Javier's way of nonviolent resistance was much more powerful, not to mention more eloquent.) We all prayed for Colombia, for an end to the killings and the poverty and the injustice, for the coming of God's reign of peace on earth, here and now, in this broken land.

Afterwards I was thrilled to meet members of the San José de Apartadó peace community, including Gildardo, the young man I helped to bring to the United States. We spoke together in Madison, Wisconsin, in 1999, and I presented him with FOR's International Peace Prize. The money for that prize, he said, helped the community buy fifteen calves. Those calves have now turned into forty cows, he said with a smile. Many of his community members have been killed. Next week marks the first anniversary of a terrible massacre that took the lives of eight community members, including Luis Eduardo Guerra, the leader I met at the SOA protest a few years ago. Javier later told me that Luis had a photo of me in his home. Gildardo said he has a photo of me too. They are my heroes — true peacemakers and Christians.

Thursday, 16 February 2006

Today brought the extraordinary opportunity of meeting village leaders from around the country, thanks to Javier Giraldo. He invited me to join their day-long meeting. Leaders from ten resistance communities had traveled for days by foot, mule, and bus to get here. They were tribal chiefs and community organizers. Several of them sat through the meeting dressed in handmade native clothes, chewing coca leaves. Coca leaves are sacred to indigenous communities in the Andes, so for them chewing the leaves is as natural as chewing gum. What a blessing to meet them and hear their stories! Hundreds of rural communities around Colombia are persecuted, but these are the most consistently targeted.

"These people identify with the persecuted Christ," Javier later told me. "They identify with Jesus as a victim of the military and the empire. They identify with Jesus, who was arrested, tortured, and killed by soldiers, just like them. And the people who were killed live on in their memory as martyrs. They have a sense that as they carry on the community life and work for peace, the martyrs come alive among them."

Javier calls these periodic meetings "an alternative university," set up so they can share with and learn from one another. We spent the morning listening to reports from each community about its situation, the paramilitary and military infiltrations, and the latest kidnappings and killings. (In order to protect them, I will not use their names.)

Meeting the Persecuted Communities

San José de Apartadó spoke about preparations to mark the first anniversary of the massacre next week. The government has been blaming the community for the massacre. Many people have left and moved to other places. The military has been taking their land by force and is now building a new military base, a fortress, nearby. The paramilitaries threaten the people when they go to town for food. They control their movements and treat them roughly. The people have been told that they have to take sides. Either they must side with the government, the paramilitaries, and the soldiers, or it will be presumed that they side with the guerrillas and therefore

88

should be killed. The people want a third option. They do not want to side with either violent group.

"Last November several peasants were in the fields collecting corn, and were shot at," one of the leaders reported. "They hid. When they came out, the soldiers threw grenades at them, then forced two dozen of them to the ground, took their tools, and shot one of them dead. The man was then dressed in guerrilla clothes and a gun was left in his hand, as if he had tried to kill the others. The army then claimed that he was a guerilla and that there had been an exchange of gunfire and they had finally killed him. Soldiers get paid according to the number of guerrillas they kill. Actually, this man was shot many times at close range. Some fifteen innocent people have disappeared, been arrested, and either imprisoned or killed. People are leaving, but we are conscious of the importance of the struggle and the need to stay together."

The next group talked about the recent fighting near their village, and the army's plan to build a new military base nearby. They have suffered ten years of massacres, but their area has been calm in recent months.

Another community told about being harassed by the army last December. After the army left, the paramilitaries came through. Both groups asked about the guerrillas. After they left, the guerrillas themselves came through, asking about the army and the paramilitaries. People continue to flee their region as well.

Another group described how the guerrillas have taken complete control of their rural area. When the paramilitaries come through, they do not look for guerrillas; they harass and massacre the people. At one time, there were fourteen thousand people in their area; sixty percent have now fled. In May 2000 the group went to the local capital and made a peace agreement with the government, but two months later, the systematic assassinations began. The group has continued to seek peaceful solutions. Recently the InterAmerican Commission for Human Rights visited them. One of the Indian leaders was captured by the army, then shot. Some people have been forced at gunpoint to become military informants. They have no choice. They tell the army that everyone in the area is a guerrilla, because that's what the army wants to hear. Meanwhile, the guerrillas demand food, and no one can say no to them without risking being killed. The community organized a demonstration against the army and sent a letter to the president. The letter was given to the head of the army, who had personally organized the violence against the community. So he came to the community, held up the letter, mocked them all, and said their letter meant nothing.

In December, the person who was giving us this report was himself arrested and imprisoned, then released. The paramilitaries told him they had orders to kill him, but they let him go as long as he promised to leave the region. If he returns, he will be killed, so now he's in Bogotá. His region has been completely taken over by the military, paramilitaries, and guerrillas. He says they are in total war. All the leaders have left. Any leader who stayed was killed. It may not be possible for this man to return. Yet the government is telling people to return to their local villages. "They are telling us to go back and be killed," this man said. Meanwhile, the paramilitaries have taken over the land that belonged to those who left. The land is not being returned, except to those who join the paramilitaries.

Another group member told similar stories about the paramilitaries, the killings, and the destruction of their indigenous villages. "Everyone is very worried," he said quietly.

A group of indigenous peoples from the mountains began their sharing by talking about their effort to retrieve their native traditions. "We need to reclaim our ancient traditions, to produce our own food, and to be strong," the leader said. "We have to recover our true identity." He was dressed head to toe in white handmade clothes. "The military has set up bases near our indigenous communities, on our sacred lands. They also fumigate our sacred places, even though there are no coca leaves there. Our people are not allowed to leave. If they try to leave, they are killed. The government put a picture of me on TV," he concluded, "saying I was a guerrilla. But none of us Indians even know how to use a gun or any weapon." He put his head down as he said this. He wasn't angry, just in a state of utter disbelief at the false accusations against him and his people.

The last community leader spoke about the huge army presence in his area. Seventeen percent of his extended community depends on the larger community for food, since they have no food in their immediate area. "But the army has prevented all movement between communities," he said, "so we cannot get food to the 17 percent of our community, and they are starving." They need food and medicine. The military has also been fumigating their region. The military base next to their village now has two thousand soldiers. They are supposed to fight the guerrillas, but instead they harass and kill the people, so the people are trying to flee. The region is also being taken over by multinational corporations, which have taken over thirty-five thousand acres in their region. The government has offered to give thousands of acres back to the community, as long as there are no guerrillas. "But we can't control the guerrillas," the leader explained, "and we are not guerrillas, so we can't get our land back. At one point, forty of us protested the main military base, so they closed the main base, and now the army roams throughout the region."

He continued, "I heard that yesterday, soldiers wearing masks beat up and kidnapped a boy. He was released later in the afternoon. Then last night, another boy and four men were disappeared. They told the first boy that if he said anything about it, they would come back and kill him. Some International Solidarity people are visiting us from Italy, and they are helping them search for the disappeared. The military apparently has orders to kidnap all eighty leaders from our region, including me," he said. "We are worried that the government wants to displace all our people and bring in more multinational corporations to take our land. The multinationals want to dig for gold, tear down the trees, and plant their own kinds of trees for lumber and paper."

The Government's Strategy

After a coffee break, one of the Bogotá activists gave a presentation on the overall strategy of the Colombian government and military. The first and most important goal is the total militarization of Colombia, he explained. They want to take over every part of the countryside through the massive presence of the army. They also want the army to have complete control of the courts and judges. They will kidnap and arrest anyone, especially the leaders, but anyone working for change. They have a massive propaganda campaign. They are telling the nation, through the media, that militarization is good for Colombia and will bring greater security — even though it doesn't. It leads to massacres, assassinations, and the total violation of human rights.

In particular, no one is allowed to be neutral, especially the so-called peace communities. You are either for the government and the armed forces or for the guerrillas. There is no other option. The government says that all "neutral" peace communities are terrorists and guerrilla bases, and it has made people around the nation believe it.

The government wants to kick out all indigenous peoples, take their land, and bring in more multinational corporations. It *wants* the displacement of whole populations so that it can take the land and give it to the corporations, so that they can all get wealthy. Meanwhile, the government promotes tourism and the idea of development, the activist explained, "when in reality, the paramilitaries control entire regions on behalf of the government, the army, and the coming multinationals. The United States makes all of this possible through the Free Trade Agreement of the Americas."

Colombia's situation is very complex — the government, the army, the paramilitaries. Sometimes they act together, sometimes not. But they are all connected with the drug dealers. Politicians are paid off by the mafia, the drug dealers, and the paramilitaries, which are technically supposed to be demobilizing, but they never do. If they leave one region, they simply appear the next day in another part of the country. Guns are never turned in. In fact, the paramilitaries are rewarded with large land grants, land stolen from the indigenous peoples. In the end, the government uses extreme aggression and violence against people and organized communities in order to steal the land for the multinational corporations under the U.S. Free Trade Agreement.

"The communities of peace are an obstacle to this government strategy," the activist said in conclusion, "so the government is trying to crush them and destroy them. These communities offer another model, another way of life, outside the government's strategy of violence, oppression, and domination. That is why they are seen as a threat."

The University of Resistance

Javier Giraldo concluded this first session with a lecture on his idea of "The University of Resistance." In 2003, twelve communities met together for the first time in San José de Apartadó to share and discuss human rights. They decided to set up this group to help teach each other about their basic rights, to create their own university of resistance. "It's for the poor, the oppressed, and the threatened," he said. "Here, knowledge is not a commodity. Our university has no titles, diplomas, students, teachers, requirements, rooms, or buildings. You don't need to read or write or be a certain age. Instead, we have a free interchange of information about how to live, farm, and build community. This is more practical. It happens in meetings like these, in our villages, and in the fields. Everyone knows something, and everyone can share something. We focus on the basic necessities of life — food, health, education, and human rights. Together we will learn alternative ways of living and give each other a vision of life."

Everyone listened attentively to Javier's vision of this underground university. They held him in great respect. He gives them hope, strength, wisdom, and vision.

Later that afternoon, Javier sent me with one of his friends for a drive through the southern, poorer half of Bogotá to see for myself the endless sprawl of shacks and rickety two-story houses, and the millions of poor people who live crowded together, barely surviving, surrounded by tall green mountains.

Tonight Javier and I had our final visit. He confessed his disappointment with the Jesuits. He has been ostracized and hated, not only by the government and its soldiers but also by other priests, bishops, and Jesuits who go about their business and ignore the killings. I told him that was my experience as well. We talked about Daniel Berrigan and Bill Bichsel, a Jesuit in Seattle imprisoned for protesting the SOA. Most Jesuits do not support our work for peace, I said, but we support him.

I asked Javier about hope. He told me about a speech he gave in Italy several years ago to a large conference on hope. He concluded that his hope must be the hope of Jesus on the cross, hope in the face of total failure, the hope that means refusing to give up one's values and to continue hoping for justice and peace, even if everything collapses around us, even if we seemingly fail. He sounds like Thomas Merton, who wrote that hope is authentic only if it looks despair in the eye and keeps on struggling for justice and peace.

Javier is one of the greatest, most faithful Jesuits I have ever met. It is a blessing to know such a saint, such a peacemaker, such a companion of Jesus. He gives me hope.

Friday, 17 February 2006

Bogotá has seven million residents, most of them barely surviving in wretched poverty, but a few living like millionaires off the backs of the poor. After my visits to El Salvador and Guatemala, I expected to see streets filled with soldiers, tanks, and machine guns. Not Bogotá. This is a new kind of war, a hidden war, based on genocide against the rural indigenous and peasants through the daily use of systematic assassination and terror, so that U.S. multinational corporations can take the land of the poor and set up shop. It's all done in secret, out of sight for the most part, far away from the hustle and bustle of Bogotá. You might never know there was a war.

Driving through Bogotá, I can see how Colombia has succeeded in its pretense of democracy. But the reality is far more sinister. Noam Chomsky calls it a "democra-tatorship." The United States overshadows every aspect of Colombia and its war. Whether through Plan Colombia, the war on drugs, or the war on terrorism, whatever it's called, the United States funds and organizes this war against the poor, the massive displacement of millions, and the unjust establishment of its multinational corporations. Whether through the sale of its weapons, the seizure of Colombia's natural resources, or the payoffs from drug dealers, the mafia, or the politicians, it reaps a fortune.

Still, parts of Bogotá were like another enchanted world. This morning Cecilia led me on a tour of the historic old-town Bogotá. We walked through Bolivar Square, saw the presidential palace, the Supreme Court, and the Congress building, and toured the cathedral. We visited St. Ignatius Church, built by the Jesuits around 1700, and walked past the old Jesuit house, which looked much like the presidential palace. These are some of the most beautiful churches I have ever seen, more beautiful than the cathedrals of Europe, relics of Spanish colonialism, with its rampage for gold and its forced conversion of the native peoples. Despite it all, the Christian artwork in the churches and the museums is astonishingly beautiful.

Later this afternoon we met the rest of our delegation and boarded a flight over the Andes to Cali, Colombia's third-largest city, where we spent the night in a hotel along the Rio Cali.

Saturday, 18 February 2006

This morning, over breakfast, Cecilia told some of us about the connection between the Catholic Church and the Colombian military. The church remains a very powerful force and ally of the Colombian government and military, she said. In spite of this alliance, dozens of priests have been killed. Some bishops and cardinals used to deliberately reassign their outspoken priests to military areas, where they would soon be assassinated. The worst was the notorious Cardinal López Trujillo, who shipped his most disruptive priests off to their deaths, and also built a shopping mall on the side, which made him rich. Instead of being kicked out of the church, he was promoted to Rome. He works in the Vatican, next to the pope, running the Office on Family Life.

Just then Bishop Leonardo Gomez, a Dominican bishop, joined us. He was attending a meeting in the hotel. He is one of only two progressive Catholic bishops in the entire country. The government has labeled him a guerrilla because of his work for peace, and recently exiled one of his priests. He has consistently met with all sides of the war in pursuit of peace, and just returned yesterday from Cuba, where he helped mediate a dialogue between the Colombian government and the ELN. He lamented the silence of the Colombian bishops in the face of so many assassinations and the ongoing repression, but he thought that over time they would change. I liked him, but I don't feel optimistic about the Catholic Church in Colombia — or in the United States.

Later this morning, Cecilia explained our upcoming journey into the region of Cauca, to the town of Santander de Quilichao, one of the centers of the drug trade, controlled by the paramilitaries. The surrounding countryside is controlled by the FARC. She reviewed our mission and the four principles of the Colombia Support Network: "peace with justice in Colombia; a negotiated solution to the conflict; strengthening of civil society; and nonalignment with armed actors." CSN works to achieve these goals through delegations, educational and media outreach, and lobbying campaigns.

Most of our delegation is from the CSN chapter in New York City, led by Patricia Dahl, who has started a sister community with the remote mountaintop village of Alto Naya, on the remote border of the southwestern departments of Cauca and the Valle del Cauca, where the government massacred scores of villagers during Holy Week, April 9-11, 2001. The government claimed that twenty-three people were killed; the villagers say as many as 140 people were killed and some six thousand displaced. After the massacre, the village split. Some remained; others fled and eventually settled on a large farm near the town of Popayán, where we will go on Monday. Some of the villagers are traveling down from the mountain on mule to meet us, a twelve-hour journey. We will meet with the survivors, learn their story, and try to advocate on their behalf with government and military officials.

So this afternoon we drove to Santander de Quilichao, a beautiful town with over eight thousand people, half of them of African descent. The parish here celebrated the first indigenous priest in the country. He started speaking out in defense of the suffering people, and was shortly thereafter assassinated on the steps of the church.

We held a long session with the leadership of the rural peace communities who together make up the Association of City Councils in northern Cauca. They told us about their years of organizing, and how they have formed their own political party. Because of their efforts, they've been persecuted, displaced, kidnapped, disappeared, and massacred. In particular, we heard horror stories about how the paramilitaries no longer kill with just guns; they use chain saws. They gather the community, pick the key people, and chop them up in front of everyone, completely terrorizing everybody. Sometimes they make the villagers perform demonic acts with the body parts of their loved ones.

"The land is sacred," one of the leaders said. "It makes us human, so we have decided not to leave the land. We will live in permanent assemblies in permanent nonviolent resistance to the war. We try to promote life, accompaniment, sharing with one another, and solidarity with other communities. Our projects help us to live. We seek self-determination. Neither the extreme right — the government and its militaries — nor the extreme left — the guerrillas — accept us. We are an obstacle to their plans. So our people are threatened and killed by both sides. We need the international community to witness what is happening and tell the world what the Colombian government is doing to its own people. In effect, the U.S. government as well has declared that indigenous people are a threat to their power.

"Daily life for the struggling people means being harassed, questioned, and perhaps kidnapped or killed by the army, the paramilitaries, or the guerrillas," he continued. "Our people try to grow crops, but they can't transport them down the mountain, so they have to use mules, which takes days and costs a fortune. We can't organize big protests because we are working full-time just to survive — to get water, food, and medicine. Meanwhile, the multinationals are moving in and taking our land."

Listening to these suffering people made it clear to me what this awful war is about. The Colombian government tells the world that the war is about the guerrillas. The U.S. government tells the world that the war is about drugs. But the innocent suffering people tell us that in reality, the war is about land. It's all about the Free Trade Agreement of the Americas. As someone said, Colombia is ground zero for globalization. This land is incredibly rich in natural resources, including oil and gold. Colombia is the entrance to the Andes and the Amazon and has access to both ocean fronts. It has the second-largest biodiversity in the world.

So the government and its armed forces move in, get rid of the people, steal their land, give it to the multinational corporations, allow them to destroy the land for whatever reason, and cover up this widespread injustice under the myth of a war on drugs. The U.S. government, weapons manufacturers, and the wealthy elite profit immeasurably from this. Meanwhile, the indigenous peoples and the peasants throughout Colombia suffer and die.

The United States is also fumigating the countryside and the rain forests, even if that means dropping toxic chemicals on helpless villagers. The goal is to terrorize these people so that they will flee their homes and be displaced. The United States has no respect for the earth either, because the fumigation actually poisons the land and the water. Again, this war is about the Free Trade Agreement of the Americas. As the prophets of old said, it is about the two great sins of idolatry: greed and violence. Only it is now on a scale the world has never seen before. From Iraq to Haiti to Colombia, the U.S. empire now pursues total greed and total violence.

Sunday, 19 February 2006

This was one of the most difficult, memorable days of my life, like days I've experienced in El Salvador, Guatemala, Nicaragua, Haiti, the Philippines, Palestine, and Iraq. At eight A.M. we boarded a "Chiva," one of those brightly colored old buses with the side walls removed so people can hop on easily. We set off for an all-day drive through the countryside on narrow dirt roads up the mountain to see various remote villages. We were following the path that the paramilitaries took during Holy Week in 2001, when they massacred the indigenous peoples of Alto Naya. We would stop along the way to hear the stories of the various killings and massacres. We could have stopped every ten yards, given the numbers of killings that happened that week alone. Unfortunately, this tour, their stories are all too common. We could have made this trip in every region, on every mountainside of Colombia.

We were setting off on a whole new kind of Stations of the Cross, stopping to hear about the kidnapping, torture, and killing of Christ in the poor by the U.S.-backed Colombian army. The paramilitaries do the dirty work for the Colombian army. A trail of blood, torture, massacres, and dead bodies — and hovering around like vultures of death, the soldiers, U.S. corporations, and U.S. military advisors.

Several villagers made the trip down the mountain on mule to accompany us, to tell us their stories, including several mothers with their children. One beautiful twelve-year-old girl, Alena Mabel, caught our attention. We all spoke with her and her little brothers and sisters, but only after several hours were we told that she was the sole witness of one particular massacre. She saw many friends and relatives chopped to pieces with chain saws. Her mother said she has never been the same.

Our first stop was at the bridge over the Rio Cauca, where over six hundred people were brutally killed in groups of twenty to thirty. The paramilitaries lined them up at the edge of the bridge, where there is a little concrete platform. The paramilitaries took them one by one, chopped off their heads with chain saws, then threw their bodies into the river. We got out and walked down to the river's edge. I looked up and saw the green mountains in the distance, several men fishing, and children running around and playing. The stories are too gruesome to imagine, but they are all too true. They symbolize the reality of Colombia.

After we passed the village of Timba, we stopped along the dirt road to meet the mayor of the village of Buenos Aires. He was a big man of African descent who told us how the paramilitaries and army soldiers had killed hundreds of people in his area, and how the U.S. corporations have now moved in to take over the region. He pointed up to the hills where the companies are currently digging for samples in search of gold. Between the Colombian government and the U.S. government, all the local communities will be displaced, killed, and eliminated, he said. The Free Trade Agreement is a great success for the United States.

We drove on, now well up into the mountains, on our one-lane dirt road dug out from along the mountainside. The cliff to our left side dropped thousands of feet below us, and it was a dangerous ride, but the view was spectacular. We looked out over hundreds of miles of green hills, deep valleys, and the distant mountains of the Andes. It reminded me of the mountains of Austria. Every fifteen minutes or so we would stop to hear a story: how the paramilitaries killed two or three people here; how they set up a checkpoint there, where they killed three or four people; how they chopped up five or six people in that house; how they killed seventeen people and threw them into the river over there.

In the distance, between the mountains, we could see the massive new hydro-electric plant and dam that the United States is building to take over the river and the valley. This particular project is the reason why these particular people were killed. There is big money involved here. Not far away, on the top of one small mountain, we saw an army barracks, with guns pointing out in every direction.

We were well up into the mountains by now, driving along the cliff, looking out at the stunning surroundings, sobered by the horrific stories we were hearing, when we came around a bend and saw up ahead an entire mountainside where all the green trees had been chopped down and the remaining area burned black. Along the roadside we saw thousands of little pine-tree seedling samples in boxes, soon to be planted by U.S. and

Canadian firms who had taken over the land to plant pine trees for their paper business. It was a scene right out of Tolkien's *The Lord of the Rings*, where the evil forces of Mordor destroyed all the forests. Here before my very eyes was globalization in action, the FTAA working to bring new products to the United States. What they don't say is that along with this new product, we support the death of the poor, the massacre of people with chain saws, and the destruction of the earth itself.

On and on we drove up the mountain and along the mountainside, stopping here and there to hear more horror stories. Once again we came around the corner to find, this time, dozens of Colombian soldiers searching a crowded bus they had stopped. Two other buses also waited to be searched. I saw the soldiers frisking the peasants, pushing them against the bus, and searching their sacks. We stopped, and the soldiers boarded our Chiva. They were serious, solemn, holding their machine guns. They wanted to know what we were doing. Cecilia introduced herself and the group, and said we had come to see the hydro-electric plant.

"Do you have permission to be here?" the commander asked. "Yes," Cecilia answered, "from Colonel Bonilla" (the head of the local military whom we would see on Wednesday). She produced letters from several U.S. senators. When he saw our letters, he let us go. "God bless you, and have a good day," he said with a smile. He looked us over, left our bus with his soldiers, then let all the other people and buses go too. They quickly boarded their Chivas and moved on. Later we learned that the military thought we were investors for a multinational corporation; that's why we were allowed to pass. They didn't want us to see their harassment of the local people. Perhaps our presence prevented the soldiers from hurting or kidnapping the people on those buses.

Later we stopped by a group of five houses and heard how the paramilitaries killed six people there as they made their way to the mountaintop of Alto Naya that Holy Week in 2001. An elderly woman appeared with her teenage son, asking for a ride. Along the way, she described how the paramilitaries stormed her house and beat her two teenage boys senseless. This boy had gone completely insane, she told us, and was in total agony, suffering headaches and hallucinations. She wanted to get him to the hospital. Tears rolled down her cheeks.

By late that afternoon we came down the mountain to the town of

Suarez, where we stopped for rice and beans, then made our way back at nightfall to Santander de Quilichao. After a day like today, I understand why Cecilia says there are two Colombias — Bogotá and the rest of the country, with its mountains, fields, countryside, poverty, death squads, dead bodies, and rivers of blood.

Monday, 20 February 2006

We drove from the beautiful town of Popayán out into the countryside to visit the farm, called "La Laguna," where half of the Alto Naya community eventually settled after the Holy Week massacre of 2001. The people found lawyers, sued the government, and somehow won the right to a new plot of land, which they eventually claimed. Over 250 survivors now live together in a communal cooperative. They walked us through the glorious fields, surrounded by mountains in the distance, showed us their crops and animals, served us a delicious lunch, and then gave us a long presentation about their life and work — and what happened to them. They spoke about their needs for school supplies, health care, clean water, housing, and agricultural assistance. They also told us about preparations for the upcoming fifth anniversary of the massacre.

"We have been together here for several years now," one of the leaders said. "Back on the mountain, they have no schools or teachers, but here we have three teachers. For the first three years, we lived in a bullfighting ring in Santander. When the government finally relented and gave us land after the lawsuit, they said only twenty families could come, but we all came and immediately started building our community. Now we grow organic coffee, corn, beans, other vegetables, and fruit, plus we raise cattle.

"We are trying to teach our young people not to give in to feelings of revenge or join the guerrillas. We want to provide new horizons for them, so we started a radio station where they could host their own radio programs."

We were crowded into a large classroom for our meeting. Everyone was present, including the children. Many of them — including most of the children — had witnessed horrific atrocities.

"Our story is long and sad," another leader said as he related the details of the Holy Week massacre of 2001. "In 2000 the paramilitaries came and started killing people near our village. Then they left and returned a few weeks later. They stole food from people coming down the mountain, set up checkpoints, took over several villages, and killed more people, throwing the bodies into the river. Some people were brought to the river, chopped into pieces, and thrown into the river. Within six months, over 350 people were killed. Then the guerrillas killed fourteen paramilitaries, so the paramilitaries started roaming through the countryside and mountainsides. The army was clearly involved in supporting the paramilitaries. They certainly did nothing to stop their killings.

"On April 9, 2001, over three hundred paramilitaries entered our area. They robbed people coming down from Alto Naya and killed a lady named Gladys by cutting her to pieces in front of everyone. On April 10 they killed five more people as they started up the mountain. They killed peasants and indigenous people who were coming down the mountain. Many were cut to pieces and never found.

"On April 11 the paramilitaries arrived on the mountaintop of Alto Naya. They walked into the few little shops and destroyed everything. They took all our food and ordered everyone to leave or be killed. Many ran away. The commander told a boy to round everyone up, to tell them there was a community meeting. As they waited in the village, they asked an Afro-Colombian man for his I.D. card. He didn't have one, so they cut him to death with machetes. He screamed out as he died, 'I'm a poor man with children. Help me!'

"When the remaining villagers arrived, the paramilitaries announced they all had five hours to leave their village or be killed. One man said, 'Let me go and get my things.' They said, 'No, you have to go now.' So they took him and killed him in front of everyone. The children saw him cut to pieces. Everyone fled immediately. Some had to run over the dead bodies. As they came down the mountain, they told everyone they met to run away quickly toward the ocean. The paramilitaries ran down the mountain after them, all the way to the sea, destroying homes and killing more people as they went. By now they were drunk, and when they got to the sea and were chasing after the people, some of them drowned. Twenty days later the army finally went up the mountain to help claim the bodies. Forty bodies were found, but over a hundred people were disappeared.

Some of the paramilitaries were arrested, but they will soon be released from prison. [They are being released by a horrific new law called the "Law of Justice and Peace," enacted by Uribe and passed by Congress, that sets all paramilitary-type criminals free.] We are deeply disturbed about this, especially the children. This war is based on terror, systematic assassination, and the displacement of peoples so that the government can take all the land and give it to the companies."

After the community leader spoke, we heard testimony from some of the women. "My name is Maria," one woman said. "My life has been filled with suffering since the day I became a widow with three children. We were so afraid. Only now do we feel the support of the community. I have joined the women's project."

"My name is Elena," another woman said. "I'm a victim of the massacre, a widow also with three children. We had to leave our home and suffer displacement. I have been here on the farm for two years now. One of the things I am learning from life is that I should not complain. With the help of the community, I've become the leader of the women's project. Our women have been in training for two years now. We have begun to make woolen handbags and sell them in town to raise money for chickens.

"Since we were born, we have been working for peace," she continued. "We did not even know what war was. But other people do not want peace. They saw us in peace, and so they did what they did."

Elena had just returned from speaking at an international conference on human rights for victims of massacres in Madrid, Spain. Every participant said they could never forgive their killers. Elena was the last person scheduled to speak, but they ran out of time. She was asked to introduce herself, so she said simply, "We forgive the people who did this to us, but we want justice, truth, and reparation." The place exploded with applause, and they asked her to speak for another forty minutes. She explained that the war in Colombia is a class war, a war for power, which is what every war is about.

She finished her testimony by looking at us and saying, "While I live, I will keep on talking." Then she sat down. I was stunned. What a courageous woman! She represents for me the best of Colombia. She models for me what it means to be a human being in such a terrible time. She has become for me a teacher of peace. I too want to forgive everyone involved in the killings, but I too want justice, truth, and reparation. I too commit myself to keep on talking.

We returned to Popayán for dinner. Popayán is magical. Every building is painted white, and brown tiles cover every roof. Green mountains surround the city. In the center, a beautiful park sets off the cathedral and the government buildings. Our hotel is around the corner from the park. People seem busy, coming and going. Children laugh. It is another world, but it too has a history of violence.

Tuesday, 21 February 2006

I was up early for a walk around Popayán. I sat in the cathedral and the park for half an hour to re-center myself in the spirit of peace after these difficult days. We spent the day in meetings, first with the grassroots progressive political party. They told us about their work to promote justice, including their campaign against a nearby university that is trying to take over large sections of land in the countryside.

This afternoon we met with the secretary to the governor of the Cauca, a kind of lieutenant governor for the state, along with his staff. Six indigenous leaders joined us. We took turns asking him questions. Señora Jimena, director of the state bureau for the displaced, answered us first. We are doing everything we can, she told us; great progress is being made, but we don't have any money, and the federal government should be doing more, et cetera, et cetera. Total baloney. Colombia is notorious for its bureaucracy, and this polite politician embodied it.

We launched into a series of specific requests on behalf of the Alto Naya people, both on the farm and up the mountain. The farm community needs a new road, food for their animals, school accreditation, police protection, and a water filter and pump. No way, we were told.

"Thank you, but with all due respect," I finally said, "we are very dissatisfied with your answers, and we will report to the senators who are following our delegation about what is going on and what is not happening. We want to make sure that no harm ever comes to these good people again, and that they get action now, beginning with a new water filter and pump this week."

"Okay," she said, looking me in the eye.

The assistant governor was worse. "We have great plans, programs, and actions," he said, sounding very much like George W. Bush. "Those people on the mountain did not have clean water before, and now they do, so their lives are better."

I couldn't take it anymore. "You cannot say they have clean water. They do not have drinkable water. We have been there. And their lives are not better now. They've lost dozens of loved ones and friends and neighbors. Their lives will never be the same. They should get clean water right now."

"It's very complicated," he kept saying. "The government, the military, the United States, the multinationals, Plan Colombia — there's not much we can do."

"Yes," I said on behalf of the group. "Of course it's complicated. Nonetheless, we want the people of Alto Naya to have a water filter, a new road, school accreditation, better security, and more support — right now." He was silenced.

Later that afternoon we had another tense meeting with the state Secretary of Education and Culture. We demanded that the farm's school be legalized, accredited, and financially supported. She kept saying no. Again we witnessed the legendary stifling bureaucracy that maintains the stagnation and keeps the war going. Every government office has a human rights division, and they write endless reports, but nothing happens except the continued violation of human rights. One member of our group said that the secretary had abandoned the community of Alto Naya. She denied it, but she also refused to do anything to support these people. And she was furious that North Americans were witnessing her hostility.

Wednesday, 22 February 2006

This morning we drove back to Cali and right into army headquarters to meet with none other than Colonel Bonilla himself, the head of the Colombian military in the department of Valle del Cauca. He was right out of the movies — charming, friendly, and slimy all at once in his green military uniform. The military compound was everything you'd imagine — high gates surrounded by armed soldiers, and outside, a long line of tearful women and children saying good-bye to their young men who were being forced into the military. The Colonel's stately office was filled with beautiful Christian art as well as helmets, miniature tanks, swords, and guns. His desk faced a four-foot-tall mahogany cross. On one table stood a two-foot-tall statue of the baby Jesus with his arms outstretched. On another table there was a large open Bible. Clearly this man is a Christian. He believes he serves Jesus by running the army, waging war, and killing the enemy. Completely blind, he does not see that he crucifies Christ all over again.

We sat down and peppered him with questions about the Alto Naya community. When he realized how serious we were, he took us to a larger meeting room and called in his staff, including his human rights officer, to rebuke our complaints. They must not have many international visitors. Our presence, along with letters from several U.S. senators, put them on the defensive.

After another twenty minutes, the Colonel decided he needed to put us at ease, so he called in the people who really are in charge — two U.S. military advisors, the men who orchestrate the entire Colombian military in this region. "The U.S. knows everything we do," he said as he introduced the U.S. soldiers, Major Dave Mellars and Colonel Valenciaz, both in U.S. army uniforms.

"We're here to assist," Dave said. "This war is different from the war in Afghanistan or El Salvador. We are limited in what we can do." I suppose he meant that he couldn't start massive bombing raids. He was limited to one killing at a time.

Major Dave Mellars. This guy was right out of central casting, like Rambo personified — young, big, bright, clean-cut, enthusiastic, articulate, efficient, energetic — and lethal. He was so gung ho. He had a big smile and plenty of down-home talk about "eliminating the enemy," "fulfilling our mission," and "getting the job done." He spoke Spanish fluently because of his experience as a Christian missionary in Uruguay years before. He was so good, and his work was pathologically demonic. He emulated Nazi efficiency, the all-American soldiers who committed atrocities in My Lai. He was like our advisors who outlined the genocide in Guatemala and El Salvador.

"The army is trying to restore peace," he said, speaking now on behalf of the Colonel. "We are trying to bring democracy." Pat (Dahl) asked him why, if that was the case, the soldiers were putting on masks, entering villages, and terrorizing the people. The Colonel denied it at first, but eventually admitted it.

"We have 250,000 people in the army," the Colonel said, offering a figure twice as large as anything we had heard. "It is almost impossible to guarantee security everywhere.

"But we are a new army," he continued. "We are developing courses in human rights and international law. The army is now one hundred percent committed to human rights. I promise that these violations will not happen again, and if anything happens, it will be investigated."

I left the place in a daze, shaking from the experience. We did what we could, at least, to let them know that we are watching them and the suffering people of Alto Naya. We hope our presence will protect them.

The afternoon brought a beautiful antidote. We crossed town, from the center of war, to a place of peace run by one of South America's leading feminist theologians, Carmiña Navia. She and the staff of her women's center on the edge of Cali work with women and young people "to build an alternative world of justice, freedom, and happiness." After giving us a tour of their magnificent facility, which featured original paintings of neighborhood women, she sat down and spoke about her work.

"We use liberation theology and eco-feminism as a framework for all that we do," she said. "We hold workshops, community meetings, and classes. We side with the poor and seek economic, social, and political liberation. We read the Bible from the point of view of the poor. It is a utopian project, but we are trying to reconcile men and women and create a new society."

I asked her what gives her hope. "I have hope for Colombia because the women are strong. They struggle hard to keep their children alive. I have hope whenever small groups like ours work together to build a new society."

I asked her what we could do to support her work. "First of all, please denounce the U.S. support of the Colombian government. The president is a dictator with an international façade of democracy that does not coincide with reality. Tell people that the image of Colombia is not true. Second, tell the people of the United States that drug trafficking is more of a problem for your people in the United States than for us Colombians."

Thursday, 23 February 2006

My brief sojourn to Colombia has come to a close. This morning I flew to Bogotá, and now I'm on my way back to the United States. The rest of the delegation will spend two more days meeting with various government officials to plead for the people of Alto Naya, but I have to return to New Mexico to attend a long-planned Pax Christi retreat.

Looking out the window at the magnificent land below and the towering Andes in the distance, my heart is heavy, and I feel sad after all I've seen and heard. The land is beautiful, and so are the people, but the killing is horrific, demonic, and perfectly legal and normal and well-funded, thanks to the United States. I hope and pray that the killings will end, that the people of the United States will wake up to its hidden war in Colombia and stop paying for it, supporting it, and ignoring it. And I resolve to keep on storming heaven for an end to this war, and the war on Iraq, and all our war-making.

The other night I woke up in a sweat at three A.M. and was unable to go back to sleep. I was fighting tears, feeling cut to the heart, but then I recalled the wisdom of Mother Jones, who said long ago, "Don't mourn — organize." So I resolved to take action, to do what I could to help stop the war on Colombia.

I take as my model Elena, the woman we met at the finca near Popayán. She has endured the horrific death of her husband and neighbors, the displacement of her children and community, and the ongoing poverty and war, yet she stood up in front of us all and spoke of forgiveness and justice and her mission.

I want to be like her. I too forgive the killers — including my own government. But I too want justice, truth, and reparations. And as long as I am alive, I too will speak out — against this evil war, the torture and massacres, the displacement and poverty, the U.S. military aid and U.S. military advisors, the multinational corporations, the destruction of the earth and the rain forests, the silence and complicity of the church in the crimes against the people, and the systematic genocide of the indigenous peoples.

As long as I am alive, I will speak out for peace, together with my sisters and brothers in Colombia.

A Prayer for Colombia

God of peace, God of justice, God of creation, hear the cry of the displaced, the terrorized, the tortured, the assassinated, the massacred people of Colombia.* Hear the cry of the widows and orphans, the survivors, the damaged and wounded. Grant them a new day of peace with justice. Help us stop the killings now.

Disarm the government, the armed forces, the paramilitaries, and the rebels who kill your beloved people. Stop the U.S. military aid that makes the killing possible, and stop the U.S. from training and advising the Colombian government's death squads. Stop the rape and destruction of your sacred land by U.S. corporations under the myth of "free trade" and the lie of "the war on drugs."

Wake up the church so that it will speak out and resist the murderous government and the forces of death. Make it stand with the suffering people and demand justice and peace. Heal the people and the land. Give your beloved people a new future of peace and hope, food and medicine, dignity and life.

Make us all sisters and brothers who live in peace with one another, who treat one another nonviolently, with respect and dignity, that we might all be your beloved children and live in your reign of love. In the name of the crucified and risen Jesus. Amen.

---

*For further information, go to www.colombiasupport.net, or contact the Colombia Support network at P.O. Box 1505, Madison, WI 53701.

CHAPTER 14

The Road Isn't Easy

I was in the midst of a travel nightmare. I had lectured in St. Cloud, Minnesota, and the next morning at 3:30 (New Mexico time) I rode off to the airport, boarded a plane at five, and then heard the dreaded words, "Our apologies for the delay, but owing to mechanical problems . . ." And there we sat for three hours.

Airborne finally, we headed to Denver, where I promptly missed my connection. Time slowed. Lines, clerks, waiting, paperwork, squalid airport food, more lines . . . and toward afternoon I was Albuquerque-bound at last. Long after dark I began the long ride home up Route 14, New Mexico's storied "Turquoise Trail," a serpentine ribbon through the high, mountainous desert. Another hour and I'd be home.

Buoyant spirits had long ago gone under; they had given way hours before to exhaustion and irritation. And a fair amount of confusion — What possible meaning could such a frustrating day have? None that I could see. I glanced up at the tapestry of stars and managed a faint prayer for guidance and light.

My mind turned to Reverend Lawrence Martin Jenco, a neighbor of mine in Berkeley in 1989. He had come to lodge right next door after being blown about like a tumbleweed by the gales of history. He had suffered as one of the U.S. hostages in Beirut and had settled in Berkeley to recover. I came to love him and over time learned of his prayers and nonviolence and of his kidnapping and suffering.

His darkest moment was being taped head-to-toe and strapped beneath a truck, a maneuver his captors used to move him clandestinely. For ten hours they drove, from Beirut to Damascus, the air choked with dust and the road pitted and rutted. Every jounce, every lurch smashed his nose against the axle — breaking his nose over and over again.

For hours he cried out a kind of whimsical prayer: "Oh, come on, Lord! Is this really necessary? I've done my part already. A Christian, a priest, now a hostage. But tied to a truck? Is this really necessary?" (He tells this story in his memoir, *Bound to Forgive*.)

My own ordeal couldn't compare. Still, as I wended along the Turquoise Trail, my lips issued a similar prayer. "Oh, c'mon, Lord, fourteen hours in jumble and limbo. What could be the meaning of such a day?"

The Turquoise Trail is storied for its breathtaking vistas and its gorgeous brown rocks, its junipers and sagebrush, its peculiar mountains and spectacular sunsets. It bore me up seven thousand feet into frigid, rarefied air. On my right were precipices and chasms, long plunges downward to its boulders and cacti. Traffic at that time of night was sparse and cautious. But close to home I came upon a driver apparently without fear of God. He swerved madly, slowed to a crawl, then raced ahead — much of the time in the wrong lane.

Another drunk driver, I thought, one of the claims to fame of our fair state — land of enchantment, land of extremes. Last in education and first in poverty. First as well in suicide, domestic violence, drug addiction — and drunk driving. That's why I'm here, to serve and stand as best I might with the poorest of our deranged nation. The disenfranchised and marginalized, addicts included, most directly bear the penalty of a culture of war. Their poverty and brokenness and despair — it derives, to my mind, from Los Alamos and our nuclear doomsday industry, where the rich genuflect before the powers of death and turn away from those in need.

For ten miles I kept my distance behind the swerving car. Now and then the car's tires skirted the edge of the road and raised clouds of gravel and dust. And the driver did little to adjust the car's speed for the hairpin turns. Watching him, I found myself gripping my own wheel more tightly than usual. I relaxed a bit as we passed through Madrid, an artist's village near where I live, snug in a valley. But not far beyond, the road bore us high up again, twisting upon itself like our ubiquitous rattlers. Then it happened: the road turned but he didn't. The car forsook the road and sailed into the dark. At sixty miles per hour.

I was dumbstruck. Pitch black all around — and me, without a cell phone. My mind raced. Surely everyone had died. But what if they hadn't? What to do?

Amid the inner clamor arose a familiar tale. ". . . a wounded man, left half-dead in a ditch. . . . A priest happened to be going by the same road and passed him by . . ." The words of the parable of the Good Samaritan. Well, here's one priest who won't pass by, I thought to myself.

I backed up, found the skid tracks in the snow, and peered over. The car was settled far below — resting miraculously in a grove of juniper trees, not among the massive boulders typical of that terrain. Presently a car passed by and I hailed it, asking the occupants to call 911. Then I buttoned up and donned my gloves and plunged into the three-foot snowdrifts. Down I slipped toward the wreck.

At length I arrived and hauled open the door, and was met by a cloud of alcohol. There inside sat a dazed young couple, drunk and stoned, but with scarcely a scratch. The police arrived thirty minutes later, hauled the couple to their feet, and placed them under arrest. In the meantime, we found a stunned three-year-old boy, strapped in tight in the backseat, un-injured. Quite a miracle.

A happy ending of sorts, but the memory of it all still has me shaken. And I stop now and then to search for meaning. The whole maddening trip from St. Cloud to Albuquerque — delay upon delay. Perhaps the di-vine hand maneuvered events. Perhaps it put me in a position to help. For had I not been on the road, no one would have observed the car careen over. And there those three would have sat, disoriented, out of sight, until freezing temperatures overtook them, mother and father and young son. It seems the turn of events had a role for me to play; it seems I was sup-posed to be there.

Perhaps, perhaps not — but quite a story in either event, a story worth committing to paper. I write it not only to settle myself down and work through the trauma. I set it down because it strikes me as a metaphor for New Mexico. In a desperately poor state like ours, disaster plays out every day before my eyes. Broad poverty and the poor dying young. And in rich corners of the state, relentless preparations for nuclear war.

Yet among us are noble people who keep the faith, who walk the road to peace. Here Good Samaritans go beyond binding wounds. I think of

Sister Hildegarde Smith, my colleague at my parish in Cimarron, who visits the sick and homebound and runs the food pantry. Marc Page, founder of the Trinity Catholic Worker House in Albuquerque, who protests regularly at Los Alamos. Father Bill McNichols and Father John Brasher, visiting the sick at all hours, presiding at an endless number of funerals for the poor. And Pax Christi friends, taking a stand in opposition to the Iraq war. They follow closely the nonviolent, troublemaking Jesus. It is a journey that cuts across the grain of injustice, a journey that sets one proclaiming a new world. A world that funds not nuclear research but housing and health care, education and environmental cleanup, and free, full-time programs to treat addiction.

The road to peace may pose risks. Many don't make it. Some fall into ditches; some sail over edges. But it's a beautiful journey nonetheless. And my prayer is that we all follow it faithfully, come what may.

Come what may. Late that night I approached the hidden dirt road that leads four miles up to the mesa on which I live. Up ahead, the long path, never smooth and broad on a sunny day in June, had become impassable under fresh three-foot snowdrifts from the high winds. I pulled over, turned off the car's engine, slung my bag over my shoulder, and trudged three-and-a-half miles home up the mountain in ten-degree weather. Overhead, a full moon lit my way, and for the first time, I felt immensely consoled.

PART IV

Practitioners of Nonviolence

We are constantly being astonished these days at the amazing discoveries in the field of violence. But I maintain that far more undreamt of and seemingly impossible discoveries will be made in the field of nonviolence.

MAHATMA GANDHI

Christians and all those who hate injustice are obligated to fight it with every ounce of their strength. They must work for a new world in which greed and selfishness will finally be overcome.

IGNACIO ELLACURÍA

CHAPTER 15

Dr. King's Daring Nonviolence

Martin Luther King Jr. was a holy prophet sent by the God of peace and justice to call our nation to repent of the sins of war, racism, greed, and nuclear weapons and to return to the new life of justice, nonviolence, and peace.

On April 3, 1968, the night before he was assassinated, Dr. King told thousands of people at the Mason Temple in Memphis, Tennessee, "For years now, we have been talking about war and peace. But now, no longer can we just talk about it. It is no longer a choice between violence and nonviolence. It's nonviolence or nonexistence."

Nonviolence or nonexistence. That is the choice before us, according to the holy prophet of the God of peace. These are the last words of Martin Luther King Jr. to the people of the world, a gauntlet he threw down before us, challenging us to reclaim the wisdom of nonviolence. Few talk about his active nonviolence anymore, but it remains his central teaching, as well as the key to all great peacemakers. All these years later, his words still sum up the critical choice facing each one of us individually and the whole world collectively.

Dr. King was an apostle of nonviolence. He wants all of us — individually, personally, nationally, and globally — to become people of nonviolence. Like Jesus of Nazareth and Mahatma Gandhi, he insists that nonviolence is the highest calling of humanity.

How do we become people of nonviolence? What did he mean by nonviolence? How do we define nonviolence? I think we need to define this clumsy, challenging word for ourselves, to discuss it with family and friends, and seek new ways to practice it in our lives and to make it central to all we do in our churches, communities, and movements.

Dr. King taught that active nonviolence begins with the vision of a reconciled humanity, the reign of God in our midst, what he called "the beloved community," the truth that all life is sacred, that we are all equal sisters and brothers, all children of the God of peace, already reconciled, all one, already united. Once we accept this vision of the heart, we can never hurt any other human being, much less remain silent while our country wages war, maintains nuclear weapons, executes people, or allows millions to starve to death.

For King, active nonviolence is much more than a tactic or a strategy; it is a way of life. We renounce violence and vow never to hurt anyone ever again. Nonviolence is not passive. It is active love and truth that seeks justice and peace for the whole human race and resists systemic evil, and persistently reconciles with everyone, and insists that there is no cause, however noble, for which we support the killing of a single human being. Instead of killing others, we are willing to be killed in the struggle for justice and peace. Instead of inflicting violence on others, we accept and undergo suffering without even the desire to retaliate with further violence as we pursue justice and peace for all people on the planet.

Nonviolence is active, creative, provocative, a life force, Gandhi said, that when harnessed becomes contagious and can disarm nations and change the world, a force more powerful than all the weapons of the world. Nonviolence always works, King insisted. If we keep experimenting with it, as Dr. King did, our lives will be transformed, and we will join the global movement to create a new world of justice and peace.

The world says there are only two options in the face of violence: fight back or run away. Nonviolence offers a third option: creative, active, peaceful resistance to injustice. We stand up publicly and resist injustice with creative love, trusting in the God of peace. Nonviolence begins in our hearts, as we renounce the violence inside ourselves, and then practice active nonviolence toward our families, communities, churches, cities, nation, and the world. We practice it personally in the face of violence and join the international grassroots movement of nonviolence for justice and peace. As we engage creative nonviolence on the national and international level, we transform the world. Dr. King exemplified this methodology of social change by marching into Birmingham and bringing down the segregation laws. Gandhi showed the power of nonviolence in his campaign for India's independence, as did the People Power movement in the Philippines and the campaign to abolish South Africa's apartheid. Through demonstrations and marches, boycotts and fasts, strikes and civil disobedience, creative nonviolence forces those who uphold systemic injustice and war to change their ways.

"The ultimate weakness of violence," Dr King once said, "is that it is a descending spiral, begetting the very thing it seeks to destroy. Instead of diminishing evil, it multiplies it. Through violence you murder the hater, but you do not murder hate. In fact, violence merely increases hate. Returning violence for violence multiplies violence, adding deeper darkness to a night already devoid of stars. Darkness cannot drive out darkness; only light can do that. Hate cannot drive out hate; only love can do that."

In this new, post-9/11, postmodern world of total violence, as the U.S. pursues war and occupation in Iraq and Afghanistan, nuclear brinkmanship, unprecedented corporate greed, and global economic and imperial domination, institutionalized nonviolence on an equally unprecedented scale remains the only hopeful way forward. Our government, the Pentagon, its war-makers, and corporate rulers have set out with renewed energy to control the planet on behalf of the global elite. The public by and large has been terrorized or pacified into accepting every new imperial pronouncement with passive indifference, whether that be the loss of civil liberties, the threatened use of nuclear weapons, or "regime change."

The empire would have us believe that democracy and peace have been fully realized, when instead, we have reached Orwell's world of permanent war. Nonetheless, people of faith, integrity, and conscience need to dig deeper into that revolutionary nonviolence that sows seeds for a future of peace. This revolutionary nonviolence seeks the nonviolent fall of imperial, nuclear America and the birth of a new, nonviolent, democratic society dedicated to global disarmament, justice for the world's poor, protection of creation, and peace for the whole human family. We have to take up where Dr. King left off.

Dr. King and our peacemaking ancestors gave their lives for this vision. They did not live to see it come about, but that did not stop them from sowing the seeds that continue to blossom. Like them, we have to walk the narrow path of nonviolence. We have to sow the seeds of peace and justice, knowing that one day there will be a harvest of peace and justice. This work requires withdrawing our cooperation from imperial America; resisting imperial America through steadfast, nonviolent action; building a new society within the shell of the old through constructive work for racial and economic justice; and envisioning a new world of nonviolence beyond imperial America.

Withdrawing Cooperation from Imperial America

"Noncooperation with evil is as much a duty as cooperation with good," Gandhi said, and Dr. King repeated it. Just as Gandhi concluded that noncooperation with imperial Britain was a duty for all Indians, we conclude that noncooperation with imperial America is a duty for us. Somehow we have to withdraw our cooperation more and more from the system of war, racism, nuclear weapons, economic hegemony, global oppression of the poor, imperial violence, and environmental destruction. We have to help others realize that we are an occupied people, living in the belly of the empire, so that they can withdraw their cooperation with the system of institutionalized injustice.

Our nonviolent noncooperation takes simple, concrete steps, from canceling subscriptions to the mass media that support war (*The New York Times, The Washington Post*); to boycotting the TV media that supports war; to seeking alternative sources of information; to putting away the flag; to cutting back on fuel consumption; to refusing to pay war taxes; to no longer supporting big businesses that oppress the world's poor; to urging young people not to join the military; to using solar power and alternative sources of energy; to growing in conscious awareness about the lives and struggles of disenfranchised people at home and abroad; to living conscientiously with the earth itself.

Resisting Imperial America through Nonviolent Direct Action

On February 15, 2003, one month before the latest U.S. war on Iraq started, some twelve million people marched for peace in 430 cities in sixty nations on six continents in the largest single day of protest in history. What a sign of hope that day was! Nonetheless, I think the nonviolent movement for peace and justice is just beginning. We will have to spend the rest of our lives in steadfast, creative, nonviolent action for justice and peace. None of us can do everything, but all of us can do something. All of us have to join the grassroots movements for social change. We can hold vigils, lobby, agitate, write, and speak out for peace. We can disturb the peace and demand disarmament and justice. Some can cross the line in acts of nonviolent civil disobedience to break the laws that legalize war, nuclear weapons, environmental destruction, and imperial America. But every one of us is needed. As Rosa Parks showed, every one of us can make a difference.

Dr. King's life became one long act of nonviolent resistance to unjust, imperial America; nonviolence became for him a way of life. Likewise, it needs to become a way of life for us too. Steadfast resistance to imperial America is now a moral requirement — indeed, a spiritual duty of faith if we want to remain faithful to the God of peace and justice in a world of total violence and injustice. Nonviolent resistance cannot be just a periodic fling; it must become our day-to-day work.

At the time of his death, Dr. King launched the "Poor People's Campaign," an ambitious plan to shut down the U.S. Capitol in a concerted demand for justice for the nation's poor, and to shut down the Pentagon in order to stop the Vietnam War. He was killed precisely because he offered a strategy to change the course of this nation. Just hours before he was shot, he spoke to his assistants about institutionalizing and internationalizing nonviolence. We have to take up where he left off. He was constantly dreaming of ways to oppose our nation's injustices so that a new world of justice and peace could be born. We need to take up that consistent, courageous work.

Building a New Society within the Shell of the Old

As we resist imperial America, we join the local struggle to bring justice to the poor, to secure jobs for the unemployed, housing for the homeless, food for the hungry, health care for the sick, education for our children, positive activities for our youth, and clean, safe, healthy environments for all. As we work locally for justice, we think globally and work in solidarity with the millions around the world who struggle each day to survive and demand the basic necessities of food, health care, housing, education, and dignity for everyone.

Gandhi insisted that if his people wanted independence, they had to start acting like they were free and take responsibility for their own lives, their own local communities, and their own local, concrete issues of poverty. He would not let his people wait for some glorious independence day down the road before they started to reform their nation; he demanded that everyone pitch in right now.

Dorothy Day called this constructive program "building a new society within the shell of the old." Her Catholic Worker movement today runs over 150 Houses of Hospitality where the homeless live, not as shelter clients but as family. They receive not only food and lodging but also loving-kindness and the strength to rebuild their lives.

Every one of us can serve in our local neighborhood in our region or state to bring about positive changes for the poor and disenfranchised, to transform our local community even as we seek the global transformation to come. The trick is to make the connection between our grassroots work for peace and justice and the global movement of transforming, revolutionary nonviolence. From now on, we have to connect every aspect of our lives with the lives of the world's poorest, and connect every work for peace and justice to a new vision of nonviolence for humanity and creation itself.

Envisioning a New World of Nonviolence beyond Imperial America

"Our only hope today lies in our ability to recapture the revolutionary spirit and go out into a sometimes-hostile world declaring eternal hostility to poverty, racism, and militarism," Dr. King said a year before he was killed. As he explained many times, his famous dream included not just racial equality and reconciliation but an entirely new world of nonviolence. Perhaps his acceptance speech for the Nobel Peace Prize summed up his vision best:

Nonviolence is the answer to the crucial political and moral question of our time — the need for humanity to overcome oppression and violence without resorting to violence and oppression. . . . I accept this award today with an audacious faith in the future of humankind. I refuse to accept the view that humankind is so tragically bound to the starless midnight of racism and war that the bright daybreak of peace and brotherhood and sisterhood can never become a reality. I refuse to accept the cynical notion that nation after nation must spiral down a militaristic stairway into the hell of nuclear destruction. I believe that unarmed truth and unconditional love will have the final word in reality. I have the audacity to believe that peoples everywhere can have three meals a day for their bodies, education and culture for their minds, and dignity, equality, and freedom for their spirits. I believe that one day humankind will bow before the altars of God and be crowned triumphant over war and bloodshed, and nonviolent redemptive goodwill will proclaim the rule of the land.

To pursue that vision of peace, a new world without war, poverty, injustice, or nuclear weapons, we have to pursue Dr. King's life and teachings of revolutionary nonviolence, to be sowers of love and compassion, resisters of imperial America, builders of justice and peace, visionaries who point the way toward global transformation. To do that, we must take up the journey of nonviolence with the same steadfast devotion that Dr. King demonstrated, and we must walk forward in that same spirit of bold action, creative experimentation, and visionary peacemaking. If we dare carry on his work, we can trust that the God of peace and justice will use us, just as God used Dr. King, to contribute to God's ongoing disarmament of humanity.

CHAPTER 16

The Moral Leadership of Ignacio Ellacuría, César Chávez, and Philip Berrigan

One reason for the world's violence, poverty, and wars lies in our crisis of ethics and leadership. Instead of pursuing a culture of morality, we have descended into a culture of immorality. Instead of having leadership that truly leads us toward greater disarmament, justice, and peace, we are misled, brought backward toward the dark ages of poverty, greed, and permanent war.

By "a culture of immorality," I mean the fundamental immorality of institutionalized violence that leaves two billion people hungry, homeless, destitute, ill, illiterate, and unemployed. I submit that any culture that executes its prisoners, bombs children abroad, and maintains thousands of weapons of mass destruction has descended into grave immorality. Yet today we regard these horrors as normal, legitimate, even natural.

"Moral principles have lost their distinctiveness," wrote Martin Luther King Jr. "For modern society, absolute right and absolute wrong are a matter of what the majority is doing. Right and wrong are relative to likes and dislikes and the customs of a particular community. We have unconsciously applied Einstein's theory of relativity, which properly described the physical universe to the moral and ethical realm."

Moral leadership requires a vision of peace and justice for the entire human family. This vision goes beyond our national borders to see the benefits of global peace and justice for ourselves and all people. Visionary leaders lift that vision up for all to see and then point the way forward to make that vision of peace a reality here and now. If we had authentic, moral leaders, everyone would be inspired to join the great work at hand — the task of abolishing hunger, poverty, homelessness, the death penalty, war, and nuclear weapons. Because we would be inspired, the spirit of peace would spread like a holy contagion, and justice "would roll down like waters."

Our immoral culture of violence is the natural consequence of a failure of leadership. Authentic leaders concerned with the noble principles of truth, love, justice, and peace would never lead their people to wage war, oppress the poor, or maintain nuclear weapons. They would not risk death for their people or other people. They would never adopt policies that destroy the environment. Today the culture of war, backed by its media and corporate billionaires, pulls the strings for its misleading puppet politicians to reap huge profits for the oil and weapons industries. Our "misleaders" do not pursue noble principles; they have no vision of truth, love, justice, or peace. They literally cannot imagine such a world. They certainly do not want such a world. They are happy to rake in the billions for their corporate sponsors, turn their backs on suffering humanity, and preserve their own immorality.

The greatest moral leaders in history were the prophets and saints, people like Francis of Assisi, Catherine of Siena, and Ignatius of Loyola. The last century brought death to more than one hundred million people from war and the consequences of war, but it also raised up a handful of remarkable moral leaders who sparked grassroots movements that disarmed and transformed their nations and the world, visionaries like Mahatma Gandhi, Dorothy Day, Martin Luther King, Jane Addams, Thich Nhat Hanh, Fannie Lou Hamer, Pope John XXIII, Archbishop Oscar Romero, Mother Teresa, Nelson Mandela, and Václav Havel. If we want future leaders rooted in morality, peace, and justice, we need to learn from the great moral leaders of the past and emulate their visionary work.

For more than twenty-five years I have worked across the United States with a variety of grassroots groups in pursuit of disarmament, justice, and peace. This work has taken me to soup kitchens, homeless shelters, death-row cells, and inner-city neighborhoods. It has also led me to organize hundreds of nonviolent demonstrations against war and nuclear weapons, and to cross the line in dozens of acts of nonviolent civil disobedience. I have lobbied dozens of politicians, given innumerable press conferences, stood at countless peace vigils, and been arrested more than seventy times. By and large, my efforts have been ignored by the media, the government, and the churches, but that has not stopped me. I realized long ago that one does the good because it is good, while the outcome is left in the hands of God.

One of the many blessings of this work has been the privilege of knowing some of the great moral leaders of our time. I would like to reflect on three of them: Ignacio Ellacuría, César Chávez, and Philip Berrigan.

Ignacio Ellacuría: Martyr for Justice

During the summer of 1985, I lived in the impoverished, war-torn Central American nation of El Salvador. Throughout the 1980s, the United States funded a brutal junta and its death squads, which killed some eighty thousand people, including Archbishop Oscar Romero, four U.S. churchwomen, and hundreds of church workers. The key leaders in the movement for peace and justice were priests at the Jesuit university in San Salvador. The president of the Jesuit university was a renowned philosopher and theologian named Ignacio Ellacuría. During the seven years prior to my visit, Ellacuría and the other Jesuits in his community received a dozen death threats a week and had their home bombed twenty-one times and shot at repeatedly. Ellacuría and his companions were targeted for death because, like Romero, they were eloquent spokesmen who denounced the injustice of turning El Salvador into a neocolonial puppet state for the United States.

The university Jesuits sent me to live and work in a church-run refugee camp for displaced people in the middle of the war zone. My job was to ask any death-squad soldier who showed up to leave.

Those were intense, terrifying, grace-filled days. I met hundreds of people who lost their loved ones, who taught me the meaning of faith, hope, and love in the midst of war and despair. But without a doubt the most inspiring figure I met that summer was Ellacuría himself. Meeting him was like meeting Ezekiel or Jeremiah. He was disturbing and challenging, as all prophets are.

When our group of five young Jesuits was brought to meet the great man in his office, he shook our hands, sat down, and said, "The purpose of the Jesuit university in El Salvador is to transform the national reality, to promote the reign of God." I was amazed. I knew right then that I was in the presence of rare courage. "However," he continued, "we have learned in El Salvador that if you are going to be for the reign of God, you have to be against the anti-reign." In other words, he said, if you want to be for peace and justice, you have to stand up publicly against war and injustice. If you want to do the good, you have to stand up publicly against institutionalized evil. If you want to create a culture of morality, you have to speak out publicly against the culture of immorality. "And so," he concluded, "we are against U.S. military aid, the U.S. bombing raids, the military dictatorship, the junta, the various death squads, the violence of the rebels, and the violence of poverty, hunger, disease, and unemployment that kills our people. We are against violence on all sides, and everyone wants to kill us."

No wonder he was in trouble. Ellacuría denounced the government's wars and injustices at every turn. Like Romero, he risked his life on behalf of the suffering Salvadoran people. He understood the consequences of his public stand for peace. Later, when his Jesuit community hosted us for a meal, we saw the bullet holes that riddled their house and heard stories of the various bombing attempts. Still, they had no intention of remaining silent in the midst of the immorality of war. They also had no intention of leaving.

A few years later, on November 16, 1989, Ellacuría and five other Jesuit priests were awoken at one in the morning, dragged outside in front of their house, forced to lie down on the grass, and shot point-blank in the head. Their brains were then removed and placed next to their bodies, a surviving Jesuit told me, to send a message to Latin America: This is what you get if you *think* about justice and peace. Twenty-six soldiers, nineteen of them trained at Georgia's "School of the Americas," a U.S. terrorist training camp, executed my Jesuit brothers.

Ellacuría embodied moral leadership. He was bold, fearless, and committed to the truth of justice and peace, so much so that he spoke not just of a new El Salvador or a new world order for the Americas, but of "the reign of God," the coming of God's realm of nonviolence for the whole human race.

Since I met Ellacuría, my life has not been the same. One cannot remain neutral or silent after encountering true moral leadership. Ellacuría teaches me that moral leadership speaks out against war and injustice, regardless of the personal consequences. He shows me that if we want to be about the public good, we have to denounce systemic evil. He models a new kind of prophetic leadership, announcing God's will of peace and justice even as politicians, military personnel, and church officials support war and injustice. Ellacuría pushes us to take a stand for peace. That is what a moral leader does. He inspires others to become moral leaders.

César Chávez: Apostle of Nonviolence

César Chávez was the founder of the United Farm Workers, but he was much more than a labor organizer. He fasted, prayed, marched, picketed, and boycotted on behalf of the poor and the day laborer, but, most interestingly, he espoused a strict nonviolence in the tradition of Mahatma Gandhi and Martin Luther King. He became one of the world's beacons of nonviolence.

César Chávez was born on March 31, 1927, into a family of farmworkers. After his father lost his farm, his family migrated from Arizona through the Southwest to California as itinerant farmers. In the 1950s, Chávez studied the Catholic Church's social teachings on the rights of workers and became a community organizer. In 1962 he founded the National Farm Workers Association with Dolores Huerta; it would later be known as the United Farm Workers. In 1965 they began a five-year boycott against grape-growers that rallied millions of supporters to the UFW. In 1968 Chávez undertook a twenty-five-day fast to reaffirm the UFW commitment to nonviolence. "For us," he said, "nonviolence is more than academic theory; it is the very lifeblood of our movement."

At the end of that famous fast, Chávez called everyone to take up the nonviolent struggle for justice. "I am convinced that the truest act of courage, the strongest act of humanity is to sacrifice ourselves for others in a totally nonviolent struggle for justice," he said. "To be human is to suffer for others. God help us to be human." Later, in the 1970s, Chávez led the largest, most successful farm strike in U.S. history, calling for a boycott of grapes, lettuce, and Gallo wine that drew the support of over seventeen million Americans.

Eventually the UFW moved their headquarters to Keene, California, and named their compound "La Paz." Pledged to voluntary poverty, Chávez never earned more than $5,000 a year. In 1984 he called for another grape boycott to protest the use of cancer-causing pesticides that killed farmworkers and their children. The boycott gained new national recognition in July 1988, when Chávez fasted for thirty-six days "as an act of penance for those who know they could or should do more."

I met Chávez in the late 1980s at a rally outside of Safeway's national headquarters in Oakland, California. He gave a stirring speech to a packed auditorium, calling for a boycott of Safeway and its grapes, and fired us up to organize the boycott. We spent the day walking door-to-door in San Francisco, urging people to boycott grapes and telling them about the dangers of pesticides for farmworkers' families. Later we gathered in the early evening to spend time with Chávez. His optimism and passion were contagious.

I saw him on several other occasions before his unexpected death in Arizona on April 22, 1993. He always spoke with enthusiasm about the boycott, the pursuit of justice, and the need for others to join the struggle. He was convinced that the boycott would succeed and that the day would come when cancer-causing pesticides would never be used again.

A few months before he died, I interviewed him for a Catholic peace journal. "I'm always hopeful," he told me. "I know it doesn't take everybody in the world to get things done. It takes a few, and those few are there. So it's not a question of converting anyone or getting people to make a new commitment. The commitments are there. We just have to find them. That's a hard thing. Getting the word out, communicating, giving people some action they can take. Together, we can make a great impact.

"We have a rule not to write or to preach about nonviolence," he continued. "I've never written a word about nonviolence. There are people like you who have written all about it. We don't have to write about it, interpret it, or dissect it. It's very simple for us. We just do it. Nonviolence has to go beyond the rhetoric. There's no real trick to being nonviolent if you're in your room praying the rosary. Anybody can do that. But how about being nonviolent in the face of violence? That's where it really happens.

"In the early days of the struggle, I talked a lot about nonviolence, more than I should have," he went on. "And so we had many people running around like saints with their hands folded together, looking like angels. So I said, 'No, you don't have to go around like you're in another world to be nonviolent. That's not the idea. Be yourselves and do things, but just don't use violence.' Nonviolence is not passivity. It requires real action. You have to get beyond the talking, writing, and planning stage and get into real action if you want to change anything. Things change when you actually confront people — as in our case, the grape industry. So it is very important to concentrate on public action for justice and peace. Without action, things are not going to change. But with action, things happen. That's my recommendation: Get involved with public action for justice and peace."

As we concluded the conversation, I asked him about his accomplishments, and his response, I think, defines commitment: "There's a difference between being of service and being a servant," he observed. "If you are of service, you serve at your convenience. You will say, 'Oh, I can't do this today at five or on Sunday, but perhaps I can next week.' If you are a servant, you are at their convenience. You are at their service all the time. You are there to serve people. That's faith and commitment."

César Chávez models active nonviolence, advocacy for the poor, selfless service, and moral leadership. Not only does he point us toward a new culture of justice for the poor; he shows us how to be human. His life and passion continue to inspire me.

Philip Berrigan: Prophet of Nuclear Disarmament

Philip Berrigan spent the final half of his life speaking out against war and nuclear weapons. As a member of the Baltimore Four and the Catonsville Nine, he led the movement against the Vietnam War and spent years in prison during the late 1960s and early 1970s. In 1973, with his wife, Elizabeth McAlister, he founded Jonah House, a community of nonviolent resistance in Baltimore, Maryland. In 1980, with his brother Daniel and the Plowshares Eight, he entered a Pennsylvania nuclear weapons plant, where he hammered on an unarmed Mark 12A nuclear nose-cone to "beat swords into plowshares." By the time of his death on December 6, 2002, Philip Berrigan had spent more than eleven years behind bars for anti-war and anti-nuclear demonstrations. He embodied prophetic, moral leadership.

I first met Philip Berrigan in 1982. I was arrested with him at many demonstrations on the East and West coasts. On December 7, 1993, Philip, Bruce Friedrich, Lynn Fredriksson, and I walked illegally onto the Seymour Johnson Air Force Base near Goldsboro, North Carolina, where we hammered on an F-15 nuclear-capable fighter bomber. For that we spent eight months together in a tiny county jail cell. Throughout those long months in jail, Phil prayed, wrote, and reflected on what he called "the moral imperative of nuclear disarmament." He showed the most single-minded commitment against nuclear weapons that I have ever witnessed. He embodied moral leadership at a time when nearly everyone ignores the nuclear peril and floats along with the tide of patriotism and war down the drain of global destruction.

"The Bomb makes every other issue redundant," Philip Berrigan told me when I interviewed him in 1992 for a peace journal. "The fact that we are complicit in the presence of the Bomb — because we help pay for it, we allow its deployment and possible use, and we have threatened to use it at least twenty-five times unilaterally during the last forty-seven years of the Cold War — destroys us spiritually, morally, psychologically, emotionally, and humanly. Our complicity in the Bomb makes us incapable of dealing with lesser social and political problems that are in reality spin-offs of our dedication to the Bomb.

"The only conversion that is real today is a conversion that accepts responsibility for the Bomb," he continued. "This conversion turns one's life around so that one is free enough to witness against this inhuman, incredibly wicked manifestation of our insanity. We all have to take responsibility for the Bomb. This conversion and responsibility will breed all sorts of life-giving, salvific benefits. They will create a just social order.

"You can't maintain a superpower status unless you're armed to the teeth. So the United States will continue with weapons development, Star Wars, and a permanent war economy, because to do otherwise is to shift the status quo and redistribute wealth. The last people who want to do that are the one/two-hundredth who control 37 percent of what the country produces, and their representatives, the president, and his official terrorists in Washington. We need to resist this business of making war. We're called to serve the poor, resist the state, and be ignored, ostracized, and sent to jail because we do that.

"Today we are condemned to being hostages of the Bomb," he said. "Legally we've been held hostage by the Bomb for years. If nuclear war breaks out, it will be legal. We'll be killed legally. That's a commentary on the law and the nature of law. But we're hopeful insofar as we are faithful. Having faith means we haven't given up on the world. Together we are part of God's reign. We live as sisters and brothers. When we believe that and live accordingly by resisting war, we generate hope.

"The disarmament of our nuclear weapons needs to be a priority for us," Phil concluded. "Peacemaking needs to be our priority. Peacemaking is not only a central characteristic of the Gospel; peacemaking is the greatest need of the world today. We are daughters and sons of God, and that means we are called to be peacemakers."

Philip Berrigan was a bright light to the nation, announcing the most unpopular but most crucial truth of our time: that if we do not disarm our nuclear arsenal and abolish war, we are doomed to destruction. He was not only a moral leader; he was a holy prophet sent by the God of peace into our culture of war. Like all prophets, he suffered harassment and imprisonment for his truth-telling, but his moral leadership was a great gift. He offered us a way out of nuclear insanity and the hope of a world without nuclear weapons. Phil would insist that each one of us must join the grassroots movement for nuclear disarmament. Otherwise our neutrality makes us complicit with the greatest immorality the world has ever known.

Philip Berrigan is one of the great inspirations of my life. He urges me to speak out against war and nuclear weapons, even if it is unpopular, even if everyone else around me is silent. If I can become a voice for nuclear disarmament and help contribute to the abolition of nuclear weapons someday in the future, it is because of Philip Berrigan.

We Can All Become Moral Leaders

In a culture of violence and war, authentic moral leadership inspires us to feed the hungry, house the homeless, educate all children, employ the unemployed, fund universal health care, abolish war, support nonviolent solutions to world conflict, and dismantle our arsenals so that we can live in peace with everyone. Moral leaders make it easier for us to be moral.

The great moral figures of history started out as ordinary people and took extraordinary chances in pursuit of the noblest causes. Ignacio Ellacuría, César Chávez, and Philip Berrigan are but three examples of moral leadership. They were visionaries of peace, champions of justice, and apostles of nonviolence. Each one of us needs to carry on their legacy and pursue these noble causes of justice, disarmament, and peace. Each one of us is called to reject violence and take up the path of active nonviolence. Each one of us can become a moral leader. If we do, we might just be able to transform our immoral culture into a culture of morality.

CHAPTER 17

Ten Nobel Peace Laureates

"We will never win a war against terror as long as the conditions for poverty and injustice remain," Archbishop Desmond Tutu said. "Poverty breeds terrorism. So we should stop spending billions on weapons of destruction and instead feed the hungry people of the world. Then we'll stop terrorism. If we want to live in peace, we have to realize we are all members of the same family."

Archbishop Tutu was just one of ten Nobel Peace Prize winners speaking to three thousand youth in Denver for the tenth anniversary of PeaceJam, an international program that brings youth from around the world together with Nobel Peace laureates — ten of them, in this case — the largest gathering ever in North America. Founded by a dynamic young couple, Dawn Engle and Ivan Suvanjieff, PeaceJam is one of the most exciting, empowering youth programs in the nation.

My friend Mairead Maguire, the Nobel laureate from Belfast whose writings I edited into the collection entitled *The Vision of Peace,* asked me to accompany her to the events. I had traveled with her before, along with our friend Adolfo Pérez Esquivel, the Nobel laureate from Argentina, to Iraq in 1999. Archbishop Tutu, the Nobel laureate from South Africa, wrote a foreword for my book *Transfiguration.*

Besides reconnecting with these heroes of mine, I got to meet José Ramos-Horta, president of East Timor; President Oscar Arias of Costa Rica; Jody Williams of the Landmines Campaign; Shirin Ebadi of Iran; Rigoberta Menchú Tum of Guatemala; and Betty Williams of Northern Ireland. And at one point during the weekend, I received a blessing from the Dalai Lama. The weekend concluded with a "Global Call to Action

134

with the Youth of the World," a plea to fight poverty, racism, environmental destruction, war, and nuclear weapons.

Such wondrously inspiring days. When the weekend was over, I drove Mairead to New Mexico, where she spoke in several churches and gave media interviews and toured Los Alamos.

It was gratifying to meet young people from around the world. At one point, before Archbishop Tutu's blessing, hundreds lined up at the microphone to say briefly what inspired them. One fifteen-year-old said, "I'm inspired by all those who stand up against the current and speak out for peace. After all, only dead fish go with the flow!"

Still, I found myself moved most by the message of the laureates.

"War doesn't work," Mairead said over and over to the thousands who had turned out. "Nuclear weapons don't work. I don't believe in a just war. The war on Iraq is totally immoral, totally illegal, and totally unnecessary. So we need to say no to war, and no to nuclear weapons. We need to learn the way of nonviolence."

Said Shirin Ebadi, the brave judge from Iran: "Every nation with nuclear weapons should dismantle them immediately. I wish, for example, that after 9/11 the U.S. had built thousands of schools in Afghanistan in honor of each victim."

José Ramos said, "I'm worried about the consequences of nuclear proliferation. I'm worried that one day we will wake to find Washington, D.C. or London destroyed by biological attacks from nonstate terrorists."

And Jody Williams asked, "What has the war and violence done in Iraq? It's only turned Iraq into a training ground for terrorists. You cannot bring change through the barrel of a gun. If we really want to disarm the world of nuclear weapons, we should begin first here at home."

"Work for peace is really hard work," she continued. "Peacemaking means getting up every single day and working hard for global peace. It's not doves or nice paintings or bad poetry; it's hard work. And that's the only way to make the world better. Peace is economic and social justice, and we have to work hard for that."

President Oscar Arias pointed out that "the United States spends over half a trillion a year on militarism, but only a tiny fraction on food, medicine, and education for the world's poor. Real security means first of all security against hunger, disease, and poverty."

And Rigoberta Menchú cut us to the core: "If there were no wars in the world, the U.S. economy would not prosper. Therefore, there must not be any more prosperity in the United States, if the world's poor are to prosper."

"World peace begins with our personal inner disarmament," the Dalai Lama taught. "We need to take seriously our religious traditions and inner life, then try to educate young people and future generations about the life of peace. And we have to recognize that all six billion of us are one."

"When I was tortured by the Argentine junta," Adolfo Pérez Esquivel told us, "I saw on the ceiling of my cell, written in blood, the words 'God does not kill.' We need to learn that lesson and resist the forces of death and destruction, and struggle for life and dignity for all. If we focus on this task, we can build peace."

Betty Williams told us flatly, "If you are not trying to change what's wrong in the world, you are part of the problem. Every one of us has a responsibility to look after humanity."

And again, Shirin Ebadi: "When you believe in your cause, you will find strength to take another step forward, and you will make a difference. One day God will ask us what we did with our lives, how we served humanity, so we better get on with that work."

"How about exporting your generosity instead of your bombs?" Archbishop Tutu concluded, as he addressed thousands of young people. "You are the future of the world. Don't become cynical like us old folks, who made a mess of the world. The world is hurting. Go and heal it."

"We need a new, nonviolent, nonkilling world. Is such a world possible? Of course it is," Mairead Maguire said. "But we have to work for it. Get to work!"

A noble mandate for all of us.

CHAPTER 18

Henri Nouwen's Spirituality of Peace

Henri Nouwen died in 1996, but he remains one of our most popular writers on the spiritual life. A man of prodigious output, he produced a sweeping catalog of books, including such titles as *Here and Now: Living in the Spirit; Life of the Beloved: Spiritual Living in a Secular World;* and *The Return of the Prodigal Son.* One might surmise that here was a strict ponderer of the inner life. Or a guide to navigating one's private relationship with God. But Nouwen's thinking surged beyond such narrow channels. Few realize the full spectrum of his spirituality.

Not that he didn't leave us a clue or two. The first emerges in his knack for walking away from positions of prestige. Quite an auspicious beginning for Nouwen — teaching assignments at Notre Dame and then the divinity schools at Yale and Harvard. But he had a conscience, and it bothered him. He knew the Gospel summons us toward "downward mobility," to solidarity with the poor. And thus he slipped off the chains of the tenure track and spent some time casting about.

He spent time with the Trappist monks in the Abbey of Genesee and then went to Peru, where he lived in a barrio. He settled finally at the L'Arche Daybreak community in Toronto, where he cared for Adam, a community member with severe disabilities. In a booklet on peace, and then later in his posthumous book, *Adam,* he wrote about Adam's ministry of peacemaking, how Adam healed him and all those around him. In this great reversal, Nouwen became the student, the disciple.

I think Henri Nouwen walked the road to peace and over time developed a beautiful spirituality of nonviolence. In 2005, *Peacework,* his masterpiece on the duty of disarmament, was finally published. There he lays out a path to peace for all of us. Nouwen wanted us to spend time in prayer, walk with Jesus, and love everyone on earth like our own sister or brother. "For Jesus," Nouwen wrote, "there are no countries to be conquered, no ideologies to be imposed, no people to be dominated. There are only children, women and men to be loved."

In the 1980s Henri and I began corresponding, something he did with thousands. Over time we became friends. In 1993 I walked onto the Seymour Johnson Air Force Base and hammered on an F-15 nuclear-capable fighter bomber, to beat swords into plowshares, as Isaiah advised. Consequently I landed in a North Carolina county jail for eight long months. Henri wrote lengthy letters of support and sent manuscripts, books, and gifts.

How grateful I was for Henri's support. He did so much to buoy my spirits and sustain my clarity. And his support stood in sharp contrast to the harsh response my "plowshares" action evoked among other church workers and theologians. His most moving gesture: his confiding that he wanted to connect his work at L'Arche with mine for peace.

Henri, it must be mentioned, built an opus of peace work in his own right. His was an inspiring journey, marked by a series of unusual and courageous steps. In the 1960s he drove through the night to join Dr. King's march from Selma to Montgomery. In the 1970s he spoke at anti-war rallies and took part in peace vigils at Connecticut's Trident submarine base. And there he hosted a weekly mass for the protestors and taught them the spiritual roots of protest.

The passing of decades did little to incline him to slow down. In the 1980s he joined hundreds of U.S. citizens on the border of Nicaragua and there protested Reagan's Contra war. He traveled to Guatemala to support the priest who succeeded martyred Father Stanley Rother. Later, he toured the United States and called for "solidarity with our crucified sisters and brothers in Central America."

When the Berrigans were in jail, Henri came to visit. He traveled deep into Nevada to join the Franciscan anti-nuclear vigils at the Nevada test site. Later he came to Washington, D.C. on the eve of the first Gulf War and denounced it before a gathering of ten thousand.

"As peacemakers, we must resist all the powers of war and destruction and proclaim that peace is the divine gift offered to all who affirm life. Resistance means saying no to all the forces of death, wherever they may be.

"Saying no is the Christian's solemn vocation," said Henri. "Just as Jesus' command to love one another cannot be seen as a part-time obligation . . . so too Jesus' call to peacemaking is unconditional, unlimited, and uncompromising. None of us is excused! Peacemaking is a full-time vocation that includes each member of God's people."

Henri had a wide-ranging mind and wrote about peace from different angles. First, he said, peacemaking begins with prayer. "Prayer is the beginning and the end, the source and the fruit, the core and the content, the basis and the goal of all peacemaking." He taught that when we pray, we enter the presence of the God of peace, the one who disarms our hearts, who bestows on us the gift of peace.

This is where political peacemaking begins. The world groans under the weight of nuclear weapons and rampant poverty and war, and they enrage and overwhelm and disorient us. All the more reason, Henri taught, to root our lives in contemplative peace. There God transforms us and deploys us to help disarm the world. In prayer we learn how to love even our enemies.

Next, he said, peacemaking begins and ends with Jesus. Jesus embodies peace, makes peace, shares peace, and blesses peacemakers. We must, therefore, become more and more like him — ourselves embodying peace, creating peace, sharing peace. "Keep your eyes on the Prince of Peace," Henri urged. We do that, he said, by focusing on Jesus, knowing him in prayer, and studying his life in the Gospels. And from there will unfold our happy mission: to carry on the works of love that he began.

Thus Henri's spirituality was a far cry from a private affair. He understood spirituality as social, political. God sends us out into the world of war to love and serve the whole human race — even those labeled as our enemies — with compassion, care, and concern. In that light, work for disarmament and justice is not a musty relic of the sixties. Nor is it the province of a few disenfranchised church people. It is integral to the life of every authentic Christian.

"Nobody can be a Christian today without being a peacemaker," Henri wrote in *Peacework*. "The bombing of Hiroshima and the nuclear arms race that followed have made peacemaking the central task for Christians. There are many other urgent tasks to accomplish — the work of worship, evangelization, healing of church divisions, alleviating worldwide poverty and hunger, and defending human rights. But all of these tasks are closely connected with the task that stands above them all: making peace. Making peace today means giving a future to humanity, making it possible to continue our life together on this planet."

Finally, Henri's spirituality of peace centered on a simple matter — our sense of "belovedness." We are the beloved sons and daughters of God, he taught over and over. The more we become aware of this, our true nature, the more we will plumb this spiritual understanding of life, the more we will reach out in love to every human on the planet. Because we are God's beloved children, we will recognize every other human being as our beloved sister or brother. When we manage that, the business of death will fall: war, poverty, injustice, nuclear weapons. All will live in God's realm of peace.

"'Blessed are the peacemakers,'" Henri said, "are the key words for Christians today."

CHAPTER 19

Denise Levertov's Peacemaking Poetry

In 1991, as the United States bombed Baghdad, the phone rang at the Jesuit community house in Oakland where I was living. It was an English professor at Stanford. Would I speak about peacemaking to her classes? she asked. Of course, I answered. In particular, she asked that I speak against the war on Iraq and help them launch a chapter of Pax Christi. Fine, I said. We spoke for several minutes more before I asked her name. "Denise Levertov," she answered.

I could scarcely believe it. One of the leading poets of the century, friend of Thomas Merton and Daniel Berrigan, Catholic convert and outspoken anti-war activist. What a thrill.

I had read her poems for years. And they never failed to entrance me and settle me into meditation and healing. So a few weeks later, when I entered her class, I was duly nervous. I needn't have been. Denise, gentle and soft-spoken, immediately put me at ease. And I launched into my talk amid a receptive crowd. Denise was my entrée to speak at Stanford on several other occasions. And I stayed in touch with her until her untimely death in 1997.

In 2006, New Directions brought out a small collection of Denise's finest poems about war and peace, *Making Peace*. Each resonates with her typical passion, nuance, and love. Part One of the volume evokes the horrors of war — Vietnam, El Salvador, the first Gulf War, the threat of nuclear annihilation. Part Two spotlights the need to protest war and injustice through nonviolent witness and action. Part Three ponders the role of poetry in such dark times as these. Part Four envisions a new world of peace. Clean, simple, close to the bone, the collection makes for excellent spiritual reading.

Denise would say it offers "a small grain of hope." I think it offers a bountiful feast. Her poem "Dom Helder Camara at the Nuclear Test Site" especially brings back memories for me. I was there, standing with Denise and Dan Berrigan in a circle with hundreds of other Christian activists in the Nevada desert, making our annual protest against nuclear weapons. Brazilian archbishop Dom Helder Camara preached to us about peace, concluding by suddenly gazing upward, begging the heavens for the gift of peace, and starting to wave up at the sky, as if to God. The whole crowd caught its breath. That gesture filled us with hope.

Some months later, Denise sent me the original draft of this poem as I languished in a North Carolina jail for my plowshares disarmament action. Hers was a gesture that deeply consoled.

> Dom Helder, octogenarian wisp
> of human substance arrived from Brazil,
> raises his arms and gazes toward
> a sky pallid with heat, to implore
> "Peace!"
> — then waves a "goodbye for now"
> to God, as to a *compadre*.
> "The Mass is over, go in peace
> to love and serve the Lord": he walks
> down with the rest of us to cross
> the cattle-grid, entering forbidden ground
> where marshals wait with their handcuffs.

These days, as the United States bombs Iraq and Afghanistan, funds Israel's oppression of Palestine, ignores the starving masses from Darfur to Haiti, and maintains thousands of nuclear weapons, we need the wisdom and consolation of Denise Levertov to inspire us.

It all boils down, she says, to "the imagination of peace":

> A voice from the dark called out,
> "The poets must give us
> imagination of peace, to oust the intense, familiar
> imagination of disaster. Peace, not only
> the absence of war."

This axiom is applicable to every war-making culture, because one of its first losses is the imagination. No one can conceive of a world without war, poverty, or nuclear weapons. But poets like Denise Levertov restore our vision. They open our minds to imagine an imponderable world, and they push us to announce that vision and make it come true:

> The choice: to speak
> or not to speak.
> We spoke.
> Those of whom we spoke
> had not that choice.

Drawing on Denise's inspiration, we too can speak out against war, poverty, and nuclear weapons and hope stubbornly for a day in which all might live in peace.

CHAPTER 20

Joan Baez: A Voice for Peace

"Come back, Woodie Guthrie, Come back, Mahatma Gandhi," sang Joan Baez in her beatific soprano. "Come back to us, Malcolm X and Martin Luther King. We're marching into Selma as the bells of freedom ring."

She's been singing for peace and civil rights for fifty years. Originally inspired by Pete Seeger, she captured the attention of the nation in the early 1960s, her politically charged music propelling her to the cover of *Time* magazine long before Bob Dylan and the Beatles. To my mind, as soon as she sang "All My Trials, Lord," the 1960s were born and the culture turned a corner. Music and politics would never be the same.

Today, she's better than ever. Her voice is strong, her vision clear, and her call for peace and justice just as urgent. She continues to use her extraordinary talent for global peace and brings the power of music to the needs of the world.

Joan Baez has long been one of my heroes. She was in New Mexico recently to perform a slew of folk songs against the latest U.S. war, including Bob Dylan's "With God on Our Side," "A Hard Rain's Gonna Fall," and "It's All Over Now, Baby Blue." She also sang "Finlandia" and a moving rendition of "Amazing Grace." *Any Day Now/Baez Sings Dylan* is my favorite of her CDs, but she has just recently released a great new CD called *Bowery Songs*, with these inspiring songs recorded live in New York.

I was thrilled that Bruce Springsteen recently recorded some of Pete Seeger's folk music and antiwar songs, and I hope Joan gets the same recognition he has. If I had any say in the matter, she'd win a place in the Rock and Roll Hall of Fame, a Lifetime Achievement Award from the Grammies, and the Nobel Peace Prize.

Joan learned from Pete Seeger and then from the writings of Gandhi to use her art for social change. She shows us that every peace and justice movement needs every possible creative outlet — music, painting, poetry, drama, film, and literature — to help uphold the vision of a new world without war, poverty, and nuclear weapons. These movements need every one of us to contribute whatever we can. In fact, everything we do should serve peace and justice, the coming of God's reign of nonviolence here on earth.

Over the years Joan has helped me with various causes and protests. Once, an envelope from her arrived at my door, and nestled inside was a large drawing she made of me speaking for peace. She's a friend and more — she's one of my teachers.

After the show I told her stories of my recent civil disobedience action against the U.S. war on Iraq, a peace walk from Thomas Merton's hermitage to Louisville to commemorate September 11, and our ongoing campaign to disarm Los Alamos. But then I grew pensive and confessed a nagging thought. The actions are necessary, I said, but they sure seem futile.

"Well, John, you know what Gandhi said, right?"

"What?"

"Full effort is full victory."

"Okay, Joan," I replied. "I'll keep at it."

Joan herself has kept at it for a long time. She walked for civil rights in the South, befriended Dr. King, sang at the 1963 March on Washington, read poetry with Thomas Merton in his hermitage, sang to Dorothy Day as she sat behind bars with the United Farm Workers, and supported dozens of movements for social change, from Poland to Chile to Nicaragua. In the seventies she ventured on a perilous trip to Vietnam, and like Daniel Berrigan and Howard Zinn, endured an interminable U.S. bombing raid.

Joan, like Berrigan, King, Merton, and Day, has a rare commitment to nonviolence. Armed only with her guitar and her voice, she helps us envision a world without war and injustice. And to make her songs authentic, she practices what she sings. She marches, organizes, gets arrested; she has refused to pay part of her taxes, and has joined countless demonstrations. A recent example of her commitment: she was the featured guest in Prague at the national birthday party in honor of Václav Havel, the heroic former president of the Czech Republic.

We can create a new world of nonviolence, she teaches, "by studying, experimenting with every possible alternative to violence on every level. By learning how to say 'No' to the nation-state, 'No' to war taxes, 'No' to military conscription, 'No' to killing in general, and 'Yes' to cooperation, to building new institutions based on the assumption that murder in any form is ruled out, by making and keeping in touch with nonviolent contacts all over the world, by engaging ourselves at every possible chance in dialogue with people to try to change the consensus that it's okay to kill."

In her famous essay "What Would You Do If?" she concluded, "The only thing that's been a worse flop than the organization of nonviolence has been the organization of violence."

These days she ends her concerts with a moving rendition of Steve Earle's hymn "Jerusalem." It rises like a prayer. Her prayer is her song, and her life is her witness. Between witness and song, she still stirs hope for peace. After all these years.

I believe there'll come a day
when the lion and the lamb
will lie down in peace together
in Jerusalem.

And there'll be no barricades then.
There'll be no wires or walls.
And we can wash all this blood from our hands,
and all this hatred from our souls.

And I believe that on that day
all the children of Abraham
will lay down their swords forever
in Jerusalem.

CHAPTER 21

Bill O'Donnell: Peacemaking Priest

My friend Father Bill O'Donnell, for twenty-five years the pastor of St. Joseph's Church in Berkeley, California, was one of the great peace and justice activists in the nation. He died suddenly on Monday morning, December 8, 2003. He had gotten up early for morning mass, had a cup of coffee, read the sports page, then gone to his desk to write his weekly bulletin announcement. Apparently he had written three sentences about the Gospel and the meaning of Advent when he fell over his desk, dead from a massive heart attack. He was seventy-three years old.

The year before, Bill spent six difficult months in a California prison for crossing the line in protest at the School of the Americas in Fort Benning, Georgia. I was with him when he was arrested that November in 2001. Bill had been arrested some 250 times in the last few decades, joining every protest against war, nuclear weapons, and injustice he could, but this was his first time in prison. Over the last ten years he had suffered from heart problems and had had a stroke. His time in prison may have hastened his end, but we were blessed to have him around as long as we did.

After his death, I spent weeks pondering our friendship, our adventures, and the lessons he taught me. I first met Bill in August 1988 in a small, poor church in the slums of San Salvador. I had flown to El Salvador with Bishop Thomas Gumbleton to offer solidarity to the struggling church workers there. One evening we were invited to a presentation about the grassroots base community movement within the church. After the talk by the frail Salvadoran priest who faced countless death threats, I was introduced to Bill. He was a big man, wearing his trademark black-leather jacket. From the start he was full of Irish wit and wisdom.

But it wasn't until I moved to Berkeley, California, the following year that we began to work together and became close. I arrived in California on August 31, 1989, to begin four years at the Graduate Theological Union in Berkeley. The next day, new friends took me to the annual vigil and protest at the Concord Naval Weapons Station, where two years earlier Brian Willson had been run over by a train carrying weapons bound for Central America. There I met Bill again, and we talked about our mutual friends and upcoming peace-movement events that he wanted me to attend.

On November 16, 1989, we were stunned by the news that six Jesuits and two women had been brutally assassinated in El Salvador. I had known and loved those Jesuits. That evening our Jesuit community in Berkeley held an open, public forum to discuss how to respond to the horrific news from El Salvador. Unexpectedly, five hundred people turned out for the event. As I entered the room, the head of the Jesuit community asked me to facilitate the forum. With no time to prepare, I welcomed everyone, suggested we break into small groups to discuss various actions we could take, and then come back together to strategize. An hour later we came up with a plan that included prayer services, press conferences, lobbying days, teach-ins, and protests.

But we decided that the main event would be a huge public service to pray for an end to U.S. military aid to El Salvador. The service would be held the following Monday morning in front of the U.S. Federal Building in downtown San Francisco. During a short break in our session, Bill walked up to the podium, introduced himself again to me, and whispered to me, "The prayer vigil is fine, but I want you to know that some of us are going to sit down in front of the Federal Building and get arrested, no matter what you plan."

I was shocked and amazed and delighted at Bill's bold announcement. He was calmly changing all our plans, and he was going to engage in civil disobedience with or without the support of the group and the Jesuits. When we gathered again, I announced that some folks were considering civil disobedience and that all those who were interested in risking arrest should stay later and plan the action. The other Jesuits in the room were shocked and appalled. Never before had a U.S. Jesuit community officially planned an event with nonviolent civil disobedience.

On Monday, November 20, 1989, over fifteen hundred people attended a public prayer service for peace in downtown San Francisco. It was a very moving event. As we concluded our last hymn, six Jesuits and two women walked up to the entrance of the Federal Building and knelt down, blocking the doorways. I expected only Bill and two or three other friends to follow us. But 120 others came forward, including fifteen other Jesuits. We were all arrested and spent the day together in a cramped jail cell. It was the largest arrest of U.S. Jesuits ever. Throughout the day, we sang and told stories. It was like a chapter out of the Acts of the Apostles. Bill later told me it was the best, most moving, most powerful demonstration he had ever attended. I agreed, and I knew that it was largely due to him.

In the years that followed, Bill and I were arrested countless times together. We were constantly in the car, driving to protests throughout California and Nevada. With our friend Dr. Davida Coady, we were arrested a dozen times at the Nevada Test Site for protesting against nuclear-weapons testing near Las Vegas. We spent over a dozen single days in jail together, usually after crossing the line at the Concord Naval Weapons Station, where U.S. bombs were being shipped to Central America.

In late 1989, two Salvadoran women, two Jesuits, and I decided to embark on a twenty-one-day fast, calling for an immediate end to U.S. military aid to El Salvador. Bill called and said that he wanted to fast with us. Our friends were concerned about his health, but he was determined. So for three long weeks, we ate nothing, drank lots of water, and prayed for a miracle of peace in El Salvador. We began the fast with a press conference and a prayer service once again in front of the San Francisco Federal Building. We ended the fast with an early morning mass at Bill's parish in Berkeley. Bill kept the fast and also kept up with all his other parish work. In the end, as we reflected on the fast, we were all surprised at what a profound spiritual experience it became for each one of us. A month later, U.S. military aid to El Salvador was cut. Eventually, a peace accord was signed.

In 1992 I went to live and work in Guatemala for the summer. Bill called to say that he was coming to visit me. For two weeks in July, we traveled through Guatemala and El Salvador with our great friends Martin Sheen, Davida Coady, and Joe Cosgrove. In El Salvador we prayed at the graves of Archbishop Romero and the martyred Jesuits, traveled to remote, poor villages, and met with church workers and local activists. On the last day, Bill celebrated a memorable mass for us in Guatemala, inspiring us to continue to stand in solidarity with our sisters and brothers in Central America.

In 1993 I was asked to coordinate the annual Good Friday peace demonstration at Lawrence Livermore Laboratories. I invited Martin Sheen and William Sloane Coffin to speak. Usually, a thousand people gathered for the rally, prayer vigil, march, and civil disobedience at the lab's entrance. During one of the weekly meetings at Bill's parish, I made an offhand, smart-alecky comment that Bill needed to get more involved in the peace movement, and that maybe he should make five hundred white crosses so that people could carry them to the entrance of Livermore. At this point Bill and I had a long-running joke between us: we'd pretend to be serious and tell one another that we each needed to do more for peace. So I didn't think anything of my jab at Bill — until the following week, when Bill announced that he had constructed one hundred large wooden crosses and painted them white. He intended to make all five hundred as his private project for Lent. On Good Friday a sea of white crosses walked to the entrance of Livermore Laboratories, where Bill, Martin, Bill Coffin, and I were arrested with nearly one hundred others who were calling for nuclear disarmament.

In 1997 I went to live and work in Northern Ireland for a year. At the end of the year, in the summer of 1998, my parents came to visit. Over the years, Bill and my parents became good friends. He once bought roses for my mother, saying that he felt sorry for her. We all laughed. As my parents and I walked through crowded Dublin, just off St. Stephen's Green, who did we run into but Bill, walking toward us, arm in arm with a woman! We were thrilled and delighted to meet him, but a little shocked to see him with someone. Then he laughed and introduced us to his sister! We sat for hours drinking coffee, laughing, and enjoying Ireland. That is a happy memory.

Bill was always in my life throughout the 1990s, at protests, parties, and other events. One of my brothers recalled meeting him at the big party after my ordination, and saying that Bill was the center of the whole day, "the life of the party." When Philip Berrigan and I were imprisoned for our plowshares disarmament action in a small North Carolina jail cell for nearly a year, Bill wrote to me every week. He scrawled his letters on his weekly church bulletins. He always pretended to be deadly serious, usually urging me to be rehabilitated, to renounce the life of crime and to stop causing so much trouble and scandal as a priest. His humor kept me sane. In the end, I dedicated my journal from jail, *Peace behind Bars,* to him and Martin Sheen.

That November of 2001, Bill still wasn't sure he would cross the line at the School of the Americas. After the mass at the Jesuit "teach-in," we had a late dinner together. Back at the hotel, he weighed the pros and cons of getting arrested. But that Sunday morning, as we prayed in front of the SOA gates, Bill felt inspired and crossed the line. He knew that he would get six months in prison for his simple action. Later, when he appeared before the notorious Georgia judge in the summer of 2002, Bill gave his now-famous statement: "Your honor, you are just a pimp for the great whore of the Pentagon."

For almost fifteen years, Bill and I had a running joke. After telling me his latest adventure — how he had denounced some nuclear weapons manufacturer, cursed some judge, or told off a grape grower who oppressed the farm workers — he would ask me, "How'm I doin'?" That was my cue to say, "Bill, you're so close. You're almost there, but not quite. Just a little bit more nonviolence, and you'll be perfect." He would break up laughing. After I was imprisoned with Phil, he wrote me a hilarious letter saying that I had become a "major prophet." That became another long running joke. Every time he visited me, I would tell him that someday he too might make it into the major leagues, but for the moment, he was still only a minor prophet. This would crack Bill up.

In August of 2003, I flew out to California to spend my forty-fourth birthday with Bill. He took me and our friends Sherry and Steve to a wonderful restaurant at the Berkeley Marina overlooking the Golden Gate Bridge. The sun was setting. We talked and laughed for hours. He told me about his experience in prison, how he taught Scripture classes daily to the other prisoners, how concerned he was about the new conservative bishop of Oakland, and how inspired he was by my new work among the poor in the New Mexico desert.

The week before he died, I wrote to tell him the news that on November 20, the local National Guard had come marching to my house and stood there shouting, "Kill! Kill! Kill!" Then I announced that someday, when he became a major prophet, the soldiers would come to his house. I knew my outrageous letter would make him laugh.

On December 8, I was sitting in my truck outside the Albuquerque airport, picking up Daniel Berrigan and two other Jesuit friends, when Davida Coady called to tell me that Bill had been found dead that morning. I was speechless, in shock. Because of Dan's visit to New Mexico and the big public retreat we had planned, I wasn't able to attend Bill's funeral. When I told Dan that Bill had been found dead at his desk, Dan said he could imagine Bill writing about the Gospel, dying, then looking up from his desk, seeing Jesus, and saying, "Hey, what are you doing here? I was just writing about you!" He would have made Jesus laugh. I am consoled imagining Jesus welcoming Bill home into paradise with open arms.

A few days later, a letter from Bill arrived. He must have mailed it a day or two before he died. I shared it with Dan. "And it came to pass that the U.S. military came to prophet John's house to wake him," the letter began, "to sing his glories, to recruit him into their chaplaincy. But in his 'John Brown' fury, the Dear pastor turned on the singing recruiters to rebuke their siren call to join them. Rebuff exacts a terrible retribution. You could be exiled back to New York for your highly anti-patriotic behavior! We'll have to stop consorting with the military, John. They may fall in love with us. Then what will we do? Your local military captain is right: you have become a huge pain in the gluteus maximus. I've got to get out to see you in a month or two, before they send you back to Georgetown to tame you."

Bill taught me many great lessons. Three come to mind as I continue to grieve the loss of my friend. First, Bill modeled "holy irreverence." He was the most irreverent, anti-clerical, anti-pompous person I have ever met, and yet he was a Catholic priest. He constantly put himself down, and in the process lifted everyone else up. It was a fine, subtle art that I used to watch with awe and admiration.

Once, while driving through the Nevada desert with him, I said to him, "Why in the world are you a priest? You are the most irreverent, most provocative, most disruptive person in the whole church." I expected a wisecrack, but was surprised when he took my question seriously. "I am a priest," he said, "because it is the best way for me to become a human being." I never forget his powerful answer. I think now that he had been pondering that question for decades. Bill learned early on to dismiss the pomp and privilege of the priesthood and spend his days in loving service to others, just like Jesus. In the process, he became whole, holy, the human being he was meant to become. That is the goal of the spiritual life — to become fully human. Bill challenges me through his holy irreverence and his holy reverence of every human being to someday become the person I am meant to be.

Second, Bill modeled "holy resistance." Bill was irrepressible. He never stopped protesting every form of violence, injustice, and war. He once told me that he tried to attend two or three vigils or protests a week. Bill understood that following Jesus while living in the belly of the beast, in the empire that our country has become, requires steadfast, public, nonviolent resistance to war, the death penalty, the oppression of workers and the poor, and our nuclear arsenal. Bill's "holy resistance" is a model not only for all church leaders but for all Christians. Bill shows us how to live in these dark times in this awful empire. From now on, every one of us has to attend weekly vigils and protests, speak out against war and injustice, and cross the line in acts of nonviolent resistance to U.S. war-making.

Finally, Bill taught me "holy humor." He was constantly laughing and making others laugh. As Dan Berrigan says, if we're going to spend our lives resisting death, we better learn to live life well along the way. Laughter is a key element in the life of Christian resistance to imperial violence. Bill didn't take himself seriously. He had a wisecrack for every occasion. He had "good crack," as the Irish say.

Perhaps it is only at his death, at the massive outpouring at his funeral, that we his friends now realize his greatness. He would laugh at this comment, but I see now that Bill was a great gift from God, not just to the Bay Area but to the whole nation. Bill was a major prophet for peace and justice. I wish more priests and Christians could learn from Bill's example and take up where Bill left off by speaking out against war and nuclear weapons and walking the path of holy irreverence to become the people of peace we are meant to be. Thanks to Bill, I intend to keep on trying.

"Dear God," Bill once wrote, "in our loneliness, comfort us. In our sorrows, strengthen us. Give us a deep faith in others, in ourselves, and in you, a bright and firm hope which will ever increase in the journey to you, who are the journey. Dare we thank you, God, for our pain, if it leads to your open embrace? Amen."

CHAPTER 22

On Retreat with Thich Nhat Hanh

"When we have peace, then we have a chance to save the planet," Thich Nhat Hanh said from the stage, sitting in the lotus position. "But if we are not united in peace, if we do not practice mindful consumption, we cannot save our planet. We need enlightenment, not just individually but collectively, to save the planet. We need to awaken ourselves. We need to practice mindfulness if we want to have a future, if we want to save ourselves and the planet."

It was August 2007, and I was in Estes Park, Colorado, in the heart of the Rocky Mountains, attending a retreat with the Buddhist leader Thich Nhat Hanh. Over a thousand people gathered for six days of silence, mindfulness, walking meditations, and talks on dharma by the legendary peacemaker.

What a blessing to be with "Thay," as he's called (a word meaning "Teacher"). I've been attending his lectures since the late 1980s, but in the late 1990s, while serving as director of the Fellowship of Reconciliation, I came to know him personally, and we became friends. Knowing Thay has been one of the great blessings of my life.

Once, in 1998, I drove from New York to Vermont to visit him, but when I arrived, I learned that he was resting, having just completed a six-day retreat with a thousand people near Boston. I was tired too, so I walked down the green lawn of the country house where he was staying, lay down under a tree, and promptly fell asleep. When I woke up a few hours later, there he was, sitting right next to me, in the full lotus position, smiling. We had a beautiful conversation about peace and nonviolence.

After another visit, I remember sitting on the floor with Thay and eight monks, in a circle, eating a delicious vegetarian pizza. We ate mindfully, peacefully, in silence. Then, after forty-five minutes, he introduced me to the monks, and we spoke about our work for peace, our mutual friends, our books, and the importance of nonviolence.

After a while he said to the group, "I feel sorry for Father John. He works so hard for peace. Could one of you please sing a song for him?" With that, one of the monks stood up and broke into an impromptu chant that went something like this: "Poor Father John. He worked so hard for peace, and then one day he died. . . . Poor Father John. He worked so hard for peace, and now he's dead." This went on for ten minutes. Afterwards, Thay and the others nodded their heads in solemn agreement. It was a classic Buddhist teaching from my Zen master: "Wake up! Life is precious! Everyone dies! Live now in the present moment!"

Thay is the epitome of gentleness. I am continually amazed at his peaceableness, how he practices so diligently what he preaches so famously. I wish I could be more like him, because in his peace I find Christ and learn more about Christ. I also wish that more Catholics, priests, nuns, Jesuits, and activists could practice peace as seriously as he does.

In 1942, when he was sixteen, Nhat Hanh entered a Buddhist monastery in rural Vietnam. Later he founded the School of Youth for Social Service, whose students rebuilt villages that were destroyed by bombs and resettled tens of thousands of people fleeing the war zones. He also founded Van Hanh Buddhist University, La Boi Press, and his own religious order of monks, the Order of Interbeing, which today has some six hundred professed monastic men and women. Many of his friends were killed during the war. He himself barely survived three separate bombings.

In 1966 the Fellowship of Reconciliation invited Thay on a three-month speaking tour of the United States. He was introduced to Thomas Merton, Daniel Berrigan, and Martin Luther King, who nominated Thay for the Nobel Peace Prize. Afterwards, Vietnam refused to let him return, so he settled in France, where he founded Plum Village, a monastic community that attracts nearly a thousand people a week. He served as chairman of the Vietnamese Buddhist Peace Delegation at the Paris Peace Talks, and he organized projects to rescue the boat people. He has authored over seventy-five books, including *Being Peace; Peace Is Every Step; No Death, No*

Fear; and *Living Buddha, Living Christ.* He has published five books a year for the last six years.

"Every breath we take, every step we make can be filled with peace, joy, and serenity," Thay writes. "We need only to be awake, alive in the present moment." He teaches the practice of mindfulness, being aware of our breathing and being centered in the present moment throughout the day — when getting up, sitting down, walking, eating, driving, talking, doing the laundry, and washing the dishes. His teaching makes the connection between the world's wars, poverty, and destruction, and the way we live our day-to-day lives, moment to moment.

"Practicing nonviolence," he once said, "is first of all to become nonviolence. . . . The essence of nonviolence is love. Out of love and the willingness to act selflessly, strategies, tactics, and techniques for a nonviolent struggle arise naturally. Nonviolence is not a dogma; it is a process. Other struggles may be fueled by greed, fear, or ignorance, but a nonviolent one cannot use such blind sources of energy, for they will destroy those involved and also the struggle itself. Nonviolent action, born of the awareness of suffering and nurtured by love, is the most effective way to confront adversity."

At this retreat I was deeply moved by Thay's "dharma talks" on the Buddha, mindfulness, breathing, sitting, walking, looking deeply, and living fully in the present moment. Afterwards I gave him the little wooden cross that I wore for years during my own talks on dharma around the country.

"You practice mindfulness, on the one hand, to be calm and peaceful," he told us one morning. "On the other hand, as you practice mindfulness and live a life of peace, you inspire hope for a future of peace."

It was amazing to sit still with a thousand people for hours, with Thay on the small platform, in perfect silence. But the best part was the walking meditation. Each morning at five-thirty, Thay and the monks led over a thousand of us on a silent twenty-minute peace walk to an open field of grass surrounded by the towering Rocky Mountains, where we sat still for thirty minutes in silence to watch the sun rise. Then we walked back to the main hall for our guided meditation.

"When we walk mindfully, we enjoy every step we take," he told us. "Every step brings freshness, relaxation, calm, and happiness. Each step is

nourishing and healing. We begin to walk like the Buddha." Thay is teaching me how to walk the road to peace, how to follow Jesus more peacefully, how to live in the Holy Spirit of peace.

One morning, as we walked slowly around the corner of one of the
buildings at the park's conference center, we came upon two enormous
elks, standing solemnly just twenty yards from us. One of them, a bull elk,
had spectacular antlers, perhaps four or five feet tall. A thousand of us, led
by Thay, walked right by them. We walked slowly, mindfully, peacefully,
one step at a time, in perfect peace. The giant elks stood there, taking it all
in, looking at us, also practicing perfect mindfulness and peace. In the distance, as a layer of white clouds hung just below the mountaintops, the
sun rose. It was a magical moment, an experience of peace, thanks to Thay
and the God of peace, to which I'll return in days to come.

CHAPTER 23

Sophie Scholl and the White Rose

It will probably come as no surprise to you, but I'm a fan of movies with a message about justice and peace — films such as *Gandhi*, *The Mission*, *In the Name of the Father*, *Missing*, *Born on the Fourth of July*, *Babette's Feast*, *Dead Man Walking*, *Erin Brockovich*, *Silkwood*, *Cry Freedom*, *Philadelphia*, *North Country*, *Testament*, *Veronica Guerin*, and *Thirteen Days*. One of my favorites is called simply *Sophie Scholl*.

Sophie who? It's the name of a German film about one of the great heroes, saints, and martyrs of the last century, a twenty-one-year-old university student in Munich who, with her brother Hans and their medical-student friends, formed a nonviolent resistance group called the White Rose Society. The group undertook to counter Nazi propaganda. They sprayed anti-Nazi graffiti around Munich and distributed outlawed leaflets on the sly.

At noon on February 18, 1943, Sophie and Hans walked into the University of Munich with a briefcase full of leaflets and, moving fast among the empty halls, distributed them where students would find them. On the way out, Sophie pushed a stack of leaflets over a balcony. They fluttered down upon the noontime crowd and thus gave the pair away. They were arrested and jailed, interrogated and tried — and upon sentencing almost immediately beheaded.

Ten years ago, historians discovered the transcripts of the interrogation and trial. The movie recreates the scene: the insidious interrogation, Sophie's artful dodging, and finally one of the most "kangaroo" of all kangaroo courts — the Nazi judge conducting the prosecution, the defense lawyers remaining mute, the verdict and sentence both foregone conclusions. From the start, the judge heaped abuse upon Sophie and thundered against her for demoralizing the troops, abetting the enemy, and undermining patriotism.

The film, starring Julia Jentsch, is worth tracking down. Study it and pray over it, for it dwells on the human response to a culture of war. It demonstrates the ideal reaction to a culture, like our own, bent on destruction and death. No large leap, then, to imagine that the film pertains to our own war-making — in Iraq, Afghanistan, Colombia, Iran, and Los Alamos.

The film challenges us to ask ourselves some serious questions. What are we going to do in the face of rapid militarism and blind patriotism? How seriously do we want to follow the nonviolent Jesus? What does courage mean for us? What price are we willing to pay to defend life and uphold God's reign of peace?

The scene in the Nazi courtroom, rooted in sheer evil and blind hatred, chills the blood. The milieu is dark, sinister, with no one willing to defend Sophie or her brother. Still, Sophie and Hans stand before their rabid condemners with great dignity. They denounce state violence. They call the stacked courtroom to renounce their allegiance to the war-making state and to seek God.

In one of their leaflets they boldly declared, "We will not be silent. We are your bad conscience. The White Rose will not leave you in peace." Their boldness refuses to dim in court. Sophie turns to the ominous judge, like Stephen before the Sanhedrin, and says, "You will soon be standing where I am now." In response, the judge explodes with rage, and Sophie and Hans, along with their friend Christoph, receive a sentence of death. They are beheaded within the hour.

Moments before, a sympathetic guard arranges for Sophie to meet with her parents. Tears flow, but there is no condemnation. Instead, they hold her and tell her how proud they are; they urge her to keep her eyes on Jesus. She thanks them for their bravery, and urges them to do the same.

Today, with thirty-five wars being waged, twenty-five thousand nuclear weapons standing ready, fifty thousand children dying of starvation every day, and the environment close to catastrophe, we wonder what we can do. Sophie and Hans didn't do much; they simply wrote and distributed a few anti-Nazi leaflets. On the other hand, they did everything they could, the most anyone could do: they gave their lives resisting the culture of war. They followed the nonviolent Jesus to the very end.

I wonder how we might aspire to the same heights. I think that Sophie and Hans would summon us to join a local peace group, hold peace vigils, distribute leaflets, write letters to the editor, speak out publicly against U.S. war-making, demand that the troops come home now, even commit nonviolent civil disobedience and accept the consequences — in other words, do what needs to be done, even in the face of no apparent result, but trusting in the goodness of our action, the rightness of our cause, the urgency of public response. Sophie would want us to sow seeds of peace for a future that is not ours, a harvest of peace we may not live to see.

My friend Howard Zinn, the great historian and author of *A People's History of the United States,* visited Santa Fe in 2006, and a luncheon was given in his honor. He had been studying social change for more than thirty-five years, he said, and he had come to a conclusion. Every U.S. movement for social change — for abolition, for suffrage, for labor rights, for civil rights, for an end to war — from its beginning, throughout its existence, and right up to the very end was . . . hopeless. I found this oddly consoling.

Howard said the key was that ordinary people kept doing ordinary acts of nonviolent resistance every day, even when there was absolutely no evidence of any positive outcome — and what's more, that that was precisely what those in power feared the most: a movement of ordinary Americans that would not go away.

Great breakthroughs of hope derived from this, he said. Change evolved because ordinary people kept at it. They refused to give up. They did what they could, no matter how small the act. Everyone involved made a difference.

This is the lesson of Sophie Scholl. Her life and witness, along with that of all the other heroes of the White Rose, bore good fruit after all. Their memory urges us to stand up and do what we can to stop the evil U.S. war on Iraq, the unjust oppression of the Palestinians, the criminal bombing of Afghanistan, the lethal funding of Colombian death squads, the demonic maintenance of our nuclear arsenal, and the refusal to feed and serve the starving masses in Africa, Latin America, India, and elsewhere.

Every one of us can do something; indeed, the nonviolent Jesus calls every one of us to do something for suffering humanity. Sophie Scholl still shines a bright light in a dark world. She inspires courage and urges us to stand with her. I hope and pray that during these dark times, we too can look raw power in the face and insist on truth and peace.

CHAPTER 24

Franziska and Franz Jägerstätter

Every year or so, a beautiful note arrives from Austria, from ninety-four-year-old Franziska Jägerstätter — wife of martyred Franz. Her card, full of love and blessings, bears a kind of weight. Whenever I hear from her, my small steps for peace fall into proper perspective — which is to say, they loom small.

In 1936 Franziska married Franz, a farmer, who overnight became a devout Catholic and served as the sacristan in their village church in St. Radegund, on the German border. In 1938 the Nazis rumbled into Austria, and it seemed that everyone but Franz supported the Anschluss. He dared speak openly against Hitler, and with only a handful of other Austrians, he refused conscription into the army.

Franz's orders arrived in February 1943, but he held strong despite urgings from his neighbors, his bishop, and his priest. He withstood appeal and casuistry, and arrest followed swiftly. The Nazis imprisoned him in Linz, tried him in Berlin, and on August 9, 1943, took off his head. His story remained unknown except to a handful of relatives and neighbors for nearly two decades.

Death, terrible and certain. And early. With what strength did he face it? To begin with, he had come to the same conclusion as Gandhi: that noncooperation with evil is as much a duty as cooperation with good. "It is still possible for us, even today, to lift ourselves, with God's help, out of the mire in which we are stuck and win eternal happiness — if only we make a sincere effort and bring all our strength to the task. It is never too late to save ourselves and perhaps some other soul for Christ."

And Franz imbibed the spirit of nonviolence. "As a Christian, I prefer to do my fighting with the Word of God and not with arms," he wrote.

In 1997 I made a pilgrimage to St. Radegund. I was beginning my Jesuit sabbatical year known as "tertianship," on my way to live and work in Northern Ireland. I wanted to pray at Franz's grave. I had an invitation to the Jägerstätter house, but finding the place posed a problem. I was by myself, and I didn't speak German. For hours I trudged through the village, with magnificent farmland on all sides, but no landmark or signpost pointed the way. Finally I came upon an elderly lady in her yard eating plums off a tree. "Can you tell me where the Jägerstätters live?" She smiled. "I'm Frau Jägerstätter."

She looks like Georgia O'Keefe, with the sparkling eyes of Mother Teresa, and has a warm, gentle soul filled with loving-kindness and an infectious joy. She carries herself with humility, a hint of shyness. But beneath that lies strength, a solid faith, deep peace, and a great Gospel conviction. To my mind, she is as much a saint as her martyred husband. After Franz died, she took up his job as sacristan and set about raising their three girls and keeping his memory alive.

When we met, she offered words of welcome and then showed me around. Our first stop was the old family home where Franz lived and worked, now a national museum. I walked from room to room and gazed upon the displays. I examined Franz's letters and his belongings, while Franziska and one of her daughters offered commentary, bringing Franz alive. That night Franziska opened her photo albums, and we gathered around, the family conjuring precious memories, warm and worn, story upon story.

I was on sacred ground — and with no gift to offer in return but one. I told Franziska that their story had influenced me long ago to become a priest, had goaded me into activism against nuclear weapons and war. And I told her that Franz had become a kind of icon. The Catholic peace movement holds his memory aloft. His witness has passed into timelessness and has inspired the likes of Thomas Merton, Dorothy Day, and Daniel Berrigan. Franziska glowed. Most of this was news to her.

Did you ever imagine it? I asked. That one day you would meet the pope? That you would inspire the faith of people around the world? That your home would achieve the dignity of a national museum? That pilgrims like me would flock to visit you? That Franz would be canonized?

Question after question — the poor woman could scarcely keep up. "Never," she answered. The Nazis had dispatched Franz with German finality. "I thought no one would ever know about him. I hid his letters under my mattress for decades. Then, in the early 1960s, Gordon Zahn learned of him and wrote his book *In Solitary Witness*. And that started the whole thing."

My last morning there we shared a liturgy in the village chapel. We prayed in German and in English for our families and friends, for the church and the world. And we prayed for the abolition of nuclear weapons and war. After the Eucharist, we stood in silence by Franz's humble grave.

It lies along the outside wall of the small chapel where he attended daily mass. Above it stands a typical Austrian crucifix bearing the words of Matthew's Gospel: "Whoever wishes to save his life must lose it, but whoever loses his life for my sake will find it." This was one of the most moving spiritual and liturgical experiences of my life. As I said farewell, Franziska pressed into my arms a bag of plums and apples from her yard, and some homemade bread.

Years later, on October 26, 2007, I joined five thousand others in the Cathedral in Linz, Austria, to celebrate the beatification of Franz Jägerstätter. Broadcast live on national TV throughout Austria, Germany, and elsewhere, the event was filled with consoling, inspiring, uplifting moments. The resounding applause for Franziska. The reading of the declaration. The unfurling of the huge banner featuring Franz's photograph, and the sight of dozens of bishops and cardinals standing up, looking up — at last! — to Franz. But the most moving moment was the presentation of his relics. Franziska kissed them, gave them to a cardinal for the cathedral in Linz, then wept. She knew it then. Franz no longer belonged to Austria. Now he belonged to the world. And his work was just beginning.

To my mind, this was an astonishing turn of events. In his time, church officials had heaped ridicule upon Franz's insistence that Jesus forbids us to kill. And now this turnabout, a kind of judgment against the "devout" German and Austrian Catholics who cheered the war and fought for Hitler. But more than that, the turnabout was a sign — a sign that points to the nature of sanctity, a sign of the *future* of sanctity.

In a world of total war, a world on the brink of destruction, only one kind of sanctity bears fruit — the kind that Jesus embodied and Franz embraced. Daring nonviolence that refuses to kill, no matter the pretext. Willingness to die without a trace of retaliation. Divine love for everyone, even the enemy. And public, prophetic defiance of patriotic militarism.

In an insane world, Franz points the way: refuse to fight, refuse to kill, refuse to be complicit in war-making, refuse to compromise — and pit your very self against structures of violence with all the nonviolence in your soul. This is exactly what we need: saints who inspire us to follow the nonviolent Jesus, say no to war, resist the culture of war, speak out for peace, work for justice, and combine the full mystical and political dimensions of faith.

Throughout those days of celebration, I reflected on the famous dream Franz had in 1938 that pushed him to say no to war. He dreamt of a beautiful train and huge crowds rushing to board it. Then he heard a voice saying, "This train is going to hell!" Next he saw a vision of many people suffering. He awoke terrified and told Franziska, then later wrote about it from prison. The dream, he wrote, was about Nazi patriotism, idolatry, and war-making.

But I wonder if his nightmare was about *all* patriotism, idolatry, and war-making, our global rush to violence, killing, war, and nuclear weapons. His dream describes our quiet, steady support for American imperialism, military domination, war on Iraq and Afghanistan, corporate greed, environmental destruction, and ignoring the cry of the world's poor. Franz wrote fiercely about the loss of our souls. We are losing our souls and we don't know it, he said. "I would like to call out to everyone who is riding in this train: 'Jump out before this train reaches its destination, even if it costs you your life!'"

That is what many of us are saying. Like Franz, we're trying not to get on the train to hell, even though crowds rush to board it, and we're crying out, "Don't get on this train. Don't support the culture of war. Don't make nuclear weapons at Los Alamos. Don't spend your life becoming rich while nine hundred million starve. Don't worship the flag of empire. Become a conscientious objector, a nonviolent resister, a public peacemaker, a Christian."

But what astonishes me most is that Franz didn't just reason his way to opposing an unjust war (which is what most good people conclude about him: he realized that Nazi warfare was unjust, so he refused to fight and did the right thing). I believe that Franz went much farther. With Franziska, he climbed the heights of faith, the kind that moves mountains. "He prayed all day long," one of his cellmates testified. He received daily communion, gave to those in need, spoke out as necessary, tried to teach his priests and bishops, prepared for death, and tried to do all things for the honor of God. He became a person of deep mystical prayer and made the connection between Gospel politics and Gospel spirituality. By the time of his death, I submit, Franz understood that to follow the nonviolent Jesus and give one's entire life to God meant that you could never kill, support war, or compromise with evil.

"Just as those who believe in Nazism tell themselves that their struggle is for survival," he wrote from prison, "so must we, too, convince ourselves that our struggle is for the eternal Kingdom. But with this difference: we need no rifles or pistols for our battle but, instead, spiritual weapons. . . . Let us love our enemies, bless those who curse us, pray for those who persecute us. For love will conquer and will endure for all eternity. And happy are they who live and die in God's love."

On the morning of Franz's death, Father Albert Jochmann, the pastor of Brandenburg, visited Franz in his cell, brought him communion, and heard his confession. He also offered Franz a Bible. To the priest's amazement, Franz said, "I am completely united with God, and any reading would disrupt my union with God." That day he wrote to Franziska in his last letter, "The heart of Jesus, the heart of Mary, and my heart are one, united for time and eternity."

Who dares say such a thing? The recent collection of previously unpublished letters by Mother Teresa, which I read on the plane to Austria, testifies clearly that she never felt such union with God. Few do. Franz did. It was the natural culmination of his steadfast, wholehearted pursuit of God and God's reign of peace, which required both nonviolent resistance to idolatry, empire, and war, and full-time devotion to prayer, worship, and nonviolent love. As the world's violence worsens, I think Franz will emerge as one of history's greatest saints.

Franz never gave up on the church, even though every single priest, pastor, chaplain, and bishop he knew advised him to fight for the Nazis, for the sake of his wife and children. He held his ground, felt sad, and prayed for them. On the day of his execution, Father Jochmann told Franz about an Austrian priest, Father Franz Reinisch, who had recently been executed for refusing to fight. This report consoled Franz a great deal. (Now we know that some four thousand priests were killed by the Nazis.) Like Franz, we have to reach out and convert every priest, pastor, minister, bishop, and cardinal who supports war, nuclear weapons, and patriotic imperialism to the Gospel wisdom of active love, nonviolent resistance, and steadfast peacemaking.

Because Franz Jägerstätter broke new ground, we do not have to do this work alone. Yes, we may be harassed, even arrested and imprisoned, but unlike Franz, we will not be alone. We can join and form communities of peace and justice to help each other take a stand for peace, support one another, and speak out in one voice against our nation's wars and injustices. Together we can build movements to say our "No" to the School of the Americas, the U.S. war on Iraq, the bombing of Iran, and the building of nuclear weapons at Los Alamos. And, like Franz, we can help one another plumb the mystical depths of Gospel nonviolence until we too are completely united with Jesus, Mary, and the God of peace.

"We must do everything in our power to strive toward the Eternal Homeland and to preserve a good conscience," Franz wrote from prison. "Though we must bear our daily sorrows and reap little reward in this world for doing so, we can still become richer than millionaires — for those who need not fear death are the richest and happiest of all. And these riches are there for the asking." He also offered this inspiring observation: "There have always been heroes and martyrs who gave their lives for Christ and their faith. If we hope to reach our goal someday, then we too must become heroes of the faith."

He also wrote, "If one harbors no thought of vengeance against others and can forgive everyone, he will be at peace in his heart — and what is there in all this world more lovely than peace? Let us pray to God that a real and lasting peace may soon descend upon this world."

"The crucial lesson to be learned," Gordon Zahn wrote in his preface to *In Solitary Witness,* "is that, however hopeless the situation or seemingly futile the effort, the Christian need not despair. Instead he can and should be prepared to accept and assert moral responsibility for his actions. It is always possible, as Jägerstätter wrote, to save one's own soul and perhaps some others as well by bearing individual witness against evil."

Franz Jägerstätter poses a great challenge. Are we willing to give our lives so literally to the nonviolent Jesus? Are we prepared to take up his steadfast resistance to empire? Can we "noncooperate" with militarism to such an extent that we suffer the disruption of our families, careers, and lives? Dare we obey Jesus as radically as blessed Franz and Franziska?

Abolishing war, poverty, and nuclear weapons will require the offering of our lives as never before, in complete surrender, in divine obedience to God's reign of peace and civil disobedience in response to the culture of death. But Franz and Franziska testify that the price is worth the blessing. Death may come, but vindication — and resurrection — will follow.

PART V

The Vision of Nonviolence

I see no poverty in the world of tomorrow — no wars, no revolutions, no bloodshed. And in that world, there will be a faith in God greater and deeper than ever in the past.

MAHATMA GANDHI

CHAPTER 25

The Earth Means the World to Me

A few years ago I moved into a handmade house atop a mesa in the high desert of New Mexico. The house is off the utility grid, powered by solar panels, with no potable water in the taps. It was my way of taking a deliberate step toward reconnecting with the earth.

Now and then, like a desert father, I walk the austere mesa and look out on the effects of a ravaging drought. And the connections turn in my mind — connections between global warming and war, poverty and nuclear weapons. An ancient truth comes to mind ever more vividly: "Blessed are the meek, the gentle, the nonviolent: they shall inherit the earth."

More and more, other people are making the same connections — and from that I take heart. But I'm also disheartened because the destruction of the earth is proceeding at a rate that alarms me; reports from across the world chill my heart.

Take, for example, the 2007 report from the United Nations' Intergovernmental Panel on Climate Change, a 1,572-page tome. "From the poles to the tropics," the authors said soberly, "the earth's climate and ecosystems are already being shaped by the atmospheric buildup of greenhouse gases and face inevitable, possibly profound, alteration."

The panel predicts widespread droughts in southern Europe and the Middle East, in sub-Saharan Africa, in the U.S. Southwest and Mexico, and flooding that could imperil low-lying islands and the crowded river deltas of southern Asia.

The report stressed that many of the regions facing the greatest risks were among the world's poorest. While limits on smokestack and tailpipe emissions could lower risks, vulnerable regions must make immediate changes to deal with shifting weather patterns, climatic and coastal hazards, and rising seas, the report concluded.

The report concurs with scientists around the world. A temperature rise of 3 to 5 degrees Fahrenheit over the next century will likely lead to the submersion of coasts and islands. The heating will bring about massive droughts that will kill crops and cause untold famine. Ice caps will melt further; hurricanes and typhoons will pack much stronger forces. And in the end the crisis could cause the death of millions, maybe hundreds of millions of people.

Shortly put: We are ears deep in a planetary emergency.

What to do? Everything must change. We need a culture that does not rely on fossil fuels, that does not hurt the environment, that does not poison the land, that does not use depleted uranium or dump radioactive waste, that does not test or build nuclear weapons, that seeks to feed everyone, and that protects the planet itself with new nonviolent institutions.

Some reports say we could easily manufacture electric cars with battery stations (so you stop at your local garage to get a new, recharged battery in the same time it now takes to fill up a tank). We certainly need a new mass transportation system, far less air travel, massive new energy systems that harness the power of the sun and the wind, and so much more.

But most of all we need the political will to demand change. The current Bush administration — indeed, the entire U.S. system — serves the corporate giants. These powers unto themselves look covetously upon the world's resources and wreak havoc upon the earth. They urge war on Iraq and bring in millions building nuclear weapons at Los Alamos and elsewhere. They remain numb to the starving masses. Corporate principalities and powers and their acolytes in government — they're hastening the planetary emergency.

People of faith and conscience need to demand new policies and laws that protect the earth and the earth's children and creatures. Our country should work cooperatively with all the world's nations to cut all greenhouse gases by at least 60 percent in the next thirty years.

But that means making the connections. If we care for the earth, we must abolish nuclear weapons once and for all. If we care for the earth, we must stop the war on Iraq and all wars. If we care for the earth, we must end both corporate greed and extreme poverty.

As we make these connections, we will deepen our spiritual understanding of reality and see everything as a spiritual issue, a life-and-death issue. We are not allowed to destroy the Creator's creation; we are not allowed to wreak such havoc on the earth or on God's children. We are called to practice nonviolence in every aspect of life.

Jesus says that if we go deep enough into nonviolence, we will protect the earth, love the earth, and in the process inherit the earth as a blessing. It seems an anachronism to say it, but Jesus was surely an environmentalist. His observations from contemplative reflection on creation run throughout the Gospels: "Consider the lilies of the field. . . . Learn a lesson from the fig tree. . . . Notice the ravens. . . ." This was someone who spent time in the mountains, who walked the land, who understood the basics of farming — and who could walk on water.

St. Francis understood these connections better than any disciple. He gave away his possessions, served lepers and the poor, created a community of peace, practiced nonviolence, loved his enemies, journeyed into enemy territory to meet the sultan at a time of war — and all the while slept outdoors, studied the stars, learned the name of every tree and bird, celebrated creation, and praised the Creator for it. He was meek, gentle, and nonviolent, and he inherited the earth. He died in its embrace.

We too can make these connections, like our Native American sisters and brothers, who have long respected "Mother Earth." Like the Buddhists, with their philosophy of compassion toward all sentient beings and creation itself.

My friends at the Jesuit center near Guelph, Canada, have begun a serious project to protect the earth and reflect on its spiritual teachings. My friend and fellow Jesuit Jim Profit runs a six-hundred-acre plot of land, home to a retreat center, an organic farm, and a wetlands-and-bush project. He studies the connection between Christian spirituality and ecology. Quite a creative Gospel endeavor, in my view.

Back home, as I walk the desert, ponder the night sky, feel the ground giving back the day's heat, I see the effects of global warming at my front door. And I long to make the link between Gospel nonviolence and creation. It will mean, I think, my entering ever more deeply the unity of creation. It will mean my becoming yet more in tune with nature, with all of humanity, and with the Holy. An ever-widening nonviolence, as it were. This is our common way forward, if we desire that promised blessing.

CHAPTER 26

The Wisdom of Thomas Merton

On the fifth anniversary of the September 11 terrorist attacks, which was also the one-hundredth anniversary of the beginning of Gandhi's *satyagraha* movement in South Africa, fifty of us set off on a sixty-mile walking pilgrimage from Thomas Merton's hermitage at the Trappist Abbey of Gethsemani to Louisville, Kentucky. Our destination: the downtown corner where Merton had his storied revelation, recorded in *Conjectures of a Guilty Bystander.*

"In Louisville," he writes, "at the corner of Fourth and Walnut, in the center of the shopping district, I was suddenly overwhelmed with the realization that I loved all those people, that they were mine and I theirs, that we could not be alien to one another even though we were total strangers.

"It was like waking from a dream of separateness, of spurious self-isolation in a special world. There is no way of telling people that they are all walking around shining like the sun."

In honor of both Merton and Gandhi, we gathered where Fourth and Walnut once were and professed a vow of nonviolence. We committed ourselves to the lifelong pilgrimage of Gospel nonviolence toward God's reign of peace.

I began studying Thomas Merton in 1982, the year I entered the Jesuit community, and to my amazement, Merton has continued to speak to me all through the years. In a darker world, a world gone madder than he could have imagined, I find his voice still rings with sanity, reason, faith, clarity, and hope.

A few years ago someone posed a question to the great theologian David Tracy. What is the future of theology in the United States? He answered without missing a beat: "For the next two hundred years, we'll be trying to catch up with Merton."

Merton has been a North Star to me over the years in my work for peace. He has kept me in religious life and kept me in the church. I often find myself in trouble as I pick my way along the path of justice and peace. And now and again I'm beset by discouraging times. But I fondly recall how Merton, putting his vision into words, wrote against war and racism and nuclear weapons, and how often he was in trouble himself — silenced, censored, imprimaturs withdrawn. Yet he stayed put, remained faithful, did what he could, said his prayers, and carried on. I take heart from Merton; he bore it all with love. And many look to him still — his sufferings continue to bear fruit and bear many of us up in hard times. Along the way, I have found four basic lessons on nonviolence in the teachings and example of Thomas Merton.

Lesson One: Become Contemplatives of Nonviolence

Merton based his life on prayer, contemplation, and mysticism. But here he turned down a counterintuitive avenue. He practiced contemplation not to turn an escapist's eye toward wars and dominations and imperial aggrandizements, but to discover the path toward communing with the living God and loving one another in peace.

Which is to say, Merton invites us first to become contemplatives and mystics of nonviolence. Contemplation, meditation, adoration, and communion take us into the presence of the God of peace. They teach us of the nonviolence of Jesus. In other words, the spiritual life begins with contemplative nonviolence. God disarms our hearts of inner violence and transforms us into people of Gospel nonviolence. We learn to let go of violence and resentments. Merton took this work very seriously, and he wants us to do the same. Through contemplative nonviolence, we learn to give God our inner violence and resentments, to grant clemency and forgiveness to everyone who hurts us, to move from anger and revenge and violence to compassion and mercy and nonviolence so that we radiate personally the peace we seek politically.

"The great problem is this inner change," Merton writes. "We all have the great duty to realize the deep need for purity of soul — that is to say, the deep need to be possessed by the Holy Spirit."

On his way to Asia in 1968, Merton told David Steindl-Rast that "the only way beyond the traps of Catholicism is Buddhism." And he expressed this another way: "I am going to become the best Buddhist I can, so I can become a good Catholic." That is the wisdom of Merton's contemplative life: to become like Buddhists — people of profound compassion, deep contemplative nonviolence — so that we can reclaim our Christianity, our humanity.

That is what he discovered through the revelation he had when he saw the Buddhist statues at Polonnaruwa, in Sri Lanka, shortly before he died. "Everything is emptiness and everything is compassion," he confessed in his journal.

This is what Merton meant when he wrote about Gandhi. "Gandhi's nonviolence was not simply a political tactic which was supremely useful and efficacious in liberating his people," Merton noted. "On the contrary, the spirit of nonviolence sprang from an inner realization of spiritual unity in himself. The whole Gandhian concept of nonviolent action and *satyagraha* is incomprehensible if it is thought to be a means of achieving unity rather than the fruit of inner unity already achieved."

Merton continues, "What is important in nonviolence is the contemplative truth that is not seen. The radical truth of reality is that we are all one." Merton spent his life looking for that radical truth, and he invites us to do likewise, despite the world's blindness. He wants us to plumb the inner depths of contemplative, mystical nonviolence, to explore the ontology of nonviolence, and to be transfigured into the light of peace, a beacon for all those trapped in the darkness of the culture of war.

Lesson Two: Become Students and Teachers of Nonviolence

To do that, Merton invites us also to become students and teachers of nonviolence. Merton was not just a great teacher but an eternal student. He constantly studied, learned, and searched every intellectual byway for the truth of nonviolence.

He started reading Gandhi in the 1950s. And then he reached out to peacemakers such as Daniel Berrigan, Dorothy Day, and the folks from the Fellowship of Reconciliation and PAX. What he learned he applied to the issues of the church, the monastery, and the world. I think that's what we have to do — study, learn, practice, and teach the holy wisdom of nonviolence and apply it to every area of life.

Merton learned about the uselessness of violence and the sheer idolatry — indeed, the insanity — of nuclear weapons, and he began to teach the church about the alternative of nonviolence. He had no great expectations of winning the Nobel Peace Prize or converting everyone, but he knew that he had to help teach nonviolence to the church so that it would become a new church of peace. In the early 1960s, when he began this project, he was worlds ahead of most U.S. Christians. He applied nonviolence to every area of life, including other religions and other cultures, and he began to receive the gift of peace from many quarters.

In his journals Merton sometimes referred to himself as "a professor of nonviolence," determined to teach himself, his community, the church, and the world the lessons of nonviolence. Through his writings, he broke new ground for mainstream churches, and he invites us to do the same, to plow ahead by applying nonviolence to every aspect of life in the hope that one day there will be a great harvest of peace.

Lesson Three: Become Apostles of Nonviolence

Merton also invites us to become apostles of nonviolence to a world of violence. In a famous article he wrote in 1961 for Dorothy Day and *The Catholic Worker,* he made this declaration: "The duty of the Christian in this time of crisis is to strive with all our power and intelligence, with our faith and hope in Christ, and love for God and humanity, to do the one task which God has imposed upon us in the world today. That task is to work for the total abolition of war. There can be no question that unless war is abolished, the world will remain constantly in a state of madness and desperation in which, because of the immense destructive power of modern weapons, the danger of catastrophe will be imminent and probable at every moment everywhere. The church must lead the way on the road to the nonviolent settlement of difficulties and toward the gradual abolition of war as the way of settling international or civil disputes. Christians must become active in every possible way, mobilizing all their resources for the fight against war. Peace is to be preached and nonviolence is to be explained and practiced. . . . We may never succeed in this campaign, but whether we succeed or not, the duty is evident."

Today there are thirty-five wars currently being fought, and the United States is involved in every one. According to the United Nations, some forty thousand people die every day of starvation. Nearly two billion people suffer in poverty and misery. We live in the midst of a structured, systemic institutionalization of violence that kills people through war and poverty.

From this global system comes a litany of violence — guns, executions, sexism, racism, violence against women and children, abortion, and the destruction of the environment, including the ozone layer, the rain forests, the oceans, and numerous plant and animal species. But on August 6, 1945, we crossed the line in this addiction to violence when we vaporized 130,000 people in Hiroshima and another 70,000 people three days later in Nagasaki.

Today we have about twenty-five thousand nuclear weapons, and there is no movement toward dismantling them. Instead, we increase our nuclear-weapons budget, send radioactive materials into outer space, and continue to hold the world hostage through our nuclear terrorism.

Theologian Jim Douglass once told me that Thomas Merton, alone in his hermitage in the woods, did more for peace in the 1960s than most peace activists. He used his talents, prayers, and connections to keep alive the dialogue and hope for nonviolence. Likewise, I think that wherever we are, whatever we do, we need to be involved in the nonviolent movements for peace and justice. None of us can do everything, but all of us can do something, like Merton, whether it's through prayer, writings, vigils, marching, the distributing of leaflets, protests, or civil disobedience.

On the first page of his book *Peace in the Post-Christian Era*, which was suppressed until its recent publication by Orbis Books, Merton writes, "Never was opposition to war more urgent and more necessary than now. Never was religious protest so badly needed."

I think everyone should join a church peace-and-justice group, like Pax Christi, as well as other groups like the ONE Campaign, which works on debt relief for Third World countries; the ongoing campaign to close the School of the Americas; the efforts to disarm Los Alamos; and the national campaigns to end the U.S. war on Iraq. We need to be publicly connected to the global grassroots movement to abolish war, poverty, and nuclear weapons, and in the process to become apostles of nonviolence to our violent world.

Lesson Four: Become Prophets of Nonviolence

Finally, Merton also invites us to become prophets of nonviolence. "It is my intention to make my entire life a rejection of, a protest against the crimes and injustices of war and political tyranny which threaten to destroy the whole human race and the whole world," Merton once wrote. "By my monastic life and vows I am saying NO to all the concentration camps, the bombardments, the staged political trials, the murders, the racial injustices, the violence and nuclear weapons. If I say NO to all these forces, I also say YES to all that is good in the world and in humanity."

Just as Merton learned to make his life a rejection of war by speaking out for peace, we too must make our lives a rejection of, a protest against the crimes and injustices and wars and nuclear weapons of our country and become prophets of nonviolence to the culture of violence.

Merton teaches us to break through the culture of war and denounce the lies of violence and speak the truth of peace and nonviolence. In 1968 he wrote to fellow Trappist Jean LeClerc that the work of the monastery is "not survival but prophecy" — prophecy in the biblical sense: to speak truth to power, to speak God's word of peace to the world of war, to speak of God's reign of nonviolence to the anti-reign of violence. I think that's our task too — not survival but prophecy.

"If one reads the prophets with ears and eyes open," Merton wrote to Daniel Berrigan in 1962, "then you cannot help recognizing our obligation to shout very loud about God's will, God's truth, and God's justice."

I'm sure Merton would have something to say about everything that is happening in the world today. Just as he condemned the Vietnam War and nuclear weapons and racism, I believe he would condemn the U.S. bombings, sanctions, and occupation of Iraq as a total disaster, a spiritual defeat.

Iraq is not a liberated country. It is an occupied country, and we are the imperial, military occupiers. There is no representative democracy in Iraq, nor do we intend to create one. We need the courage of Thomas Merton to speak out against this horrific war and to demand an immediate end to the U.S. war on and occupation of Iraq, the immediate return of all U.S. troops, reparations for our Iraqi sisters and brothers, and a U.N. program for nonviolent conflict resolution that can begin the healing.

But if we are to become true prophets of nonviolence like Thomas Merton, we have to speak out against every form of systemic violence. We need to say the unpopular things: end the oppression of the Palestinians; support nonviolent Israeli and Palestinian peacemakers, the Jewish vision of shalom, and human rights for Palestinians; end all U.S. military aid to and war-making in Colombia; stop all surveillance of peace and justice activists; close Guantanamo and all U.S. terrorist training camps, beginning with Fort Benning's notorious "School of Assassins"; close the CIA, the NSA, the FBI, and the Pentagon; leave the World Trade Organization; erase the entire Third World debt; distribute free medicine to everyone with HIV/AIDS; abolish the death penalty; welcome every immigrant and undocumented person; rebuild New Orleans and its levees and take care of its hurricane victims; house the homeless; grant universal health care; fund nonviolence education in every school on the planet; stop rigging elections; develop treaties for nuclear disarmament; join the World Court; obey international law; sign the Kyoto Accord; fund alternatives to fossil fuels; stop global warming; end the Star Wars program; disarm Los Alamos; cut the entire military budget; abolish every one of our nuclear weapons and all weapons of mass destruction; and then redirect those hundreds of billions of dollars toward the hard work for a lasting peace by feeding every starving child and refugee on the planet with a global Marshall Plan.

Merton teaches us, like Ezekiel and the prophets of old, that whether we are heard or not, whether our message is accepted or not, our vocation is to speak the truth of peace, to become a prophetic people who speak for the God of peace to the culture of war.

"I am on the side of the people who are being burned, bombed, cut to pieces, tortured, held as hostages, gassed, ruined, and destroyed," Merton wrote in the 1960s. "They are the victims of both sides. To take sides with massive power is to take sides against the innocent. The side I take is the side of the people who are sick of war and who want peace, who want to rebuild their lives and their countries and the world."

"It is absolutely necessary to take a serious and articulate stand on the question of nuclear war, and I mean against nuclear war," Merton wrote in the 1960s to his friend Etta Gullick. "The passivity, the apparent indifference, the incoherence of so many Christians on this issue, and worse still the active belligerency of some religious spokesmen is rapidly becoming one of the most frightful scandals in the history of Christendom."

Merton concludes his great essay "Blessed Are the Meek," which focuses on the roots of Christian nonviolence, by talking about hope, saying that our work for peace and justice is not based on the hope for results or the delusions of violence or the false security of this world, but in Christ. Our hope is in the God of peace, in the resurrection of Jesus.

Merton gives me hope, hope to become a contemplative and mystic of nonviolence and commune with the God of peace; hope to teach the wisdom of nonviolence to a culture of violence; hope to practice active nonviolence in a world of indifference; hope to speak out prophetically for peace in a world of war and nuclear weapons; hope to uphold the vision of peace, a new world without war.

In one of his letters to Daniel Berrigan, Merton offered words of encouragement: "You are going to do a great deal of good simply stating facts quietly and telling the truth. The real job is to lay the groundwork for a deep change of heart on the part of the whole nation so that one day it can really go through the *metanoia* we need for a peaceful world. So do not be discouraged. Do not let yourself get frustrated. The Holy Spirit is not asleep. Keep your chin up."

This is good advice for the times we are enduring. Don't be discouraged, don't despair, don't be afraid, don't give in to apathy, and don't give up. Become contemplatives, students, teachers, apostles, and prophets of Gospel nonviolence. Take up where Merton left off, go as deep as Merton did, stand on Merton's shoulders, and try to transform the church and the world into the community of creative, loving nonviolence.

CHAPTER 27

A World without War

The story is told that in the early 1980s a small group gathered in their church basement in East Germany to ask a daring question: "What will Germany look like a thousand years from now when the Berlin Wall finally falls?"

There was no question of the Wall coming down soon. Such a prospect was unimaginable. Communism was here to stay. The grip of the Soviet empire was permanent. The suicidal competition between the two nuclear superpowers seemed preordained.

And yet, this group asked the question. They allowed their imagination free rein. What would a world without the Wall look like? And what must we do now to hasten that great day?

I believe that asking such a question, letting our imaginations challenge us, and daring to dream of a new world unleashes a spirit of transformation that can actually change history.

According to the story, the small group felt energized as they discussed their dream. They decided to meet again a few weeks later. Soon, word of the meetings spread, and more people began to meet in church basements to dream of a world without the Wall. Over the next few years, a grassroots movement grew. Ordinary people on both sides of the Wall pursued the vision of unity and reconciliation. They met, organized, prayed, and spoke out. Then, out of the blue, Mikhail Gorbachev announced his new policy of *perestroika*. The Polish Solidarity movement pushed the Soviets out, and a new democracy was born. Events moved quickly. Communism collapsed, and the Soviet Union imploded.

The God of peace is hard at work trying to disarm the world. But God needs our help. God needs every one of us to be part of God's global transformation for peace and justice. God needs our grassroots movements of nonviolent resistance to disarm the world.

The grassroots movement begun in East Berlin by a handful of faithful dreamers made all the difference. In November 1989, tens of thousands of people marched in East Berlin to demand the fall of the Wall. Every day, more people marched. Soon, hundreds of thousands were marching. Then, all of a sudden, on November 9, the Wall fell down. It took the world by surprise. Yet the Berlin Wall could not have come down peacefully without the grassroots visionaries who met, dreamed, imagined, discussed, and organized over the years. Gorbachev needed a grassroots movement to make his vision bear fruit. In other words, the Wall fell because ordinary people imagined a world without the Wall. They held up the possibility of a world without the Wall and then acted as if such a world was possible and inevitable.

New Abolitionists

The daring vision of these people reminds me of the Abolitionists, who imagined a world without slavery. "Every human being is equal," they said. "Everyone has the right to life, liberty, and the pursuit of happiness, regardless of race. No human can be bought, owned, or sold. Therefore, slavery must be abolished — now!" They were dismissed as unpatriotic revolutionaries, unrealistic idealists, and crazy lunatics. "Slavery has always existed," they were told. "This is the way things have always been and always will be. Some people are not human. Even St. Paul endorsed slavery! You cannot change the course of history."

"No," they answered. "The time of slavery is over. A new world without slavery is coming." The great herald of the abolitionist movement, William Lloyd Garrison, set the tone for the movement when he published his newspaper, *The Liberator*, in 1831 and declared to the world that the age of slavery was over. His front-page editorial in the first issue stirred the nation. "I am in earnest. I will not equivocate. I will not excuse. I will not retreat a single inch, and I will be heard," he announced. With the help of hundreds of committed activists, Garrison wrote and spoke out day and night against slavery. He encouraged people to join the movement, smuggle slaves into Northern freedom, disrupt the culture of slavery, and demand equality for all. The Abolitionists were threatened, mobbed, attacked, jailed, and even killed. But they continued practicing steadfast, nonviolent civil disobedience against the laws that legalized slavery. Their vision and determination paved the way for the abolition of slavery.

Like the Abolitionists, who envisioned a world without slavery, we are new abolitionists who envision a world without poverty, injustice, war, and nuclear weapons. We give our lives to that vision, creating movements for disarmament and justice, trusting that one day the vision will come true.

Reclaiming Our Imaginations

We have much to learn from these imaginative visionaries. Like them, we need to reclaim our imaginations. We have to begin to dream again of new possibilities. We need to exercise our imaginations and envision a new world, no matter how crazy others think we are. In a world such as ours, that means imagining a world without war or violence.

One of the casualties of our culture of war is the loss of our imagination. We can no longer imagine a world without war or nuclear weapons or violence or poverty. Few dream of a world of nonviolence. If we do, we are dismissed as naïve or idealistic. Yet without the imagination for peace, the vision of peace, we will never get out of the downward cycle of violence that is destroying us.

If we want to discover the blessings of peace, we have to renounce war and dedicate ourselves to a new world without war. Every human being has to join this global campaign for peace if we are to lead ourselves away from the precipice of global catastrophe. We need to rediscover our shared humanity and reclaim the higher principles of love, justice, compassion, and equality. We need to demand food, clothing, housing, education, health care, and dignity for every child on the planet. We need to give our lives for a future of peace.

The Blindness of Violence

But if we want to envision such a world, we must recognize that we are blind, that we can no longer see clearly. We can no longer see our way to peace. We cannot see our way toward dismantling our arsenals, ceasing our bombing raids, supporting the world's poorer nations, ending hunger and poverty, and pursuing universal brotherhood and sisterhood. Instead, we see only war and further wars. We can imagine all kinds of weapons of mass destruction and ever-greater invasions and wars. We put our best minds, our time, our funds, and our energies into this vision of war. In the process, we blind ourselves to the vision of peace.

Violence blinds us. We think we see, but we have grown blind to our shared humanity. We do not see one another as human beings, much less brothers and sisters. Instead, we see nonhumans, aliens, outsiders, competitors, objects of class, race, or nationality. When that happens, we label people as enemies and declare them expendable.

If we want to see our way toward a new world without war, we need to recover our sight. We need to meet together in church basements and small grassroots communities to discuss a daring, provocative question: "What would a world without war look like?" As we ask the question, we can begin to imagine such a world. Then we can discuss and enact ways to make that new world a reality.

In order to reclaim this vision, we need to teach each other that war is not inevitable, that war is not our future, that nuclear destruction need not be our destiny, that peace can come true for all people. We have to rekindle the desire for the vision of peace. Once we desire it, we will pray for it, work for it, and welcome it — and move our culture from blindness to vision, from numbness to imagination, from war to peace.

Since our blind leaders are driving us to the brink of destruction, we have to take the wheel, turn back, and lead one another away from the brink. We cannot expect vision from the war-makers or their media spokespeople. Only peacemakers, people of creative, contemplative nonviolence, can see the way forward toward a world of peace.

The Lens of Nonviolence

The night before he was killed, the great visionary Martin Luther King Jr. spoke of being on the mountaintop. From that great God's-eye perspective, he pointed the way forward by calling us to choose nonviolence. He upheld a vision of humanity as "the beloved community of God." Through the practice of creative nonviolence, he argued and demonstrated, we can make that vision, that dream, come true. Through the eyes of peace, we learn to recognize every human being, including the enemy, as a child of God, and we welcome God's reign of peace in our midst. Through the lens of nonviolence, we begin to see new solutions and a way beyond the world's violence into God's realm of nonviolence — here and now, in our own lifetime.

Shortly before he died, John Lennon was asked why he devoted so much of his time and energy to peace. "Isn't that a waste of time?" the reporter asked. Lennon answered that he believed that Leonardo da Vinci helped make flying possible because he imagined it, discussed it, painted it, and brought it into people's consciousness. "What a person projects can eventually happen," Lennon said. "And therefore, I always want to project peace. I want to project it in song, word, and action. I want to put the possibility of peace into the public imagination. And I know, as certain as I am standing here, that someday peace will be."

If we dare to imagine a new world without war and reclaim the possibility of peace, as Martin Luther King Jr. and John Lennon believed, we will raise human consciousness and help pave the way toward a new, nonviolent world. Our mission, our duty, our vocation is to reclaim that vision of peace, uphold it for all to see, and pursue the abolition of war, violence, and nuclear weapons.

Living in Hope

For years, one of my friends, the legendary folksinger Pete Seeger, has questioned friends and audiences who feel hopeless. "In the early 1970s," he asks, "did you ever expect to see President Nixon resign because of Watergate?"

"No," people answer.

"Did you ever expect to see the Pentagon leave Vietnam the way it did?"

"No, we didn't," everyone answers.

"In the 1980s, did you expect to see the Berlin Wall come down so peacefully?" Pete asks.

"No, never," they respond.

"In the 1990s, did you expect to see Nelson Mandela released from prison, apartheid abolished, and Mandela become president of South Africa?"

"Never in a million years."

"Did you ever expect the two warring sides of Northern Ireland to sign a peace agreement on Good Friday?"

"Never."

"If you can't predict those things," Pete concludes, "don't be so confident that there's no hope! There's always hope!"

We do not know what the future will bring. We cannot see where the road is leading. We know the sufferings, wars, and injustices tearing us apart, but we do not know the outcome. And so we cannot presume that there is no hope of a new world of peace.

We only know our mission, our vocation, our duty is to proclaim God's reign of peace and resist the anti-reign of war.

We know that the God of peace is alive and active among the struggling people of the world. We know that if we repent of our violence and take up God's way of nonviolence, the world can be transformed into a haven of harmony for everyone. We know that if we stay on the road to peace, one day we will enter God's house of peace and meet the God of peace face-to-face.

The key, then, is to remain faithful to the journey of peace, to take the next step on the path of nonviolence, to join hands with one another and walk forward with hope. If we can do what Jesus says ("love one another," "love your enemies"), if we can live out his Sermon on the Mount and seek first God's reign of justice for the poor every day of our lives, if we can be faithful to the one who walks ahead of us, then he will give us his blessings and offer us God's reign of peace here and now.

If we keep the faith, practice nonviolence, and love one another no matter what the outcome, if we hold our heads high, as Jesus instructed his disciples, always on the lookout for the coming of the God of peace, one day our liberation from violence will come, and a new dawn of peace will rise for everyone.

If we dare to believe, if we dare to take Jesus at his word, if we put down the sword, if we act like we are true disciples, apostles, and prophets of the nonviolent Jesus, if we ask God for the gift of God's reign, then one day there will be no more war, no more nuclear weapons, no more hunger, no more poverty, no more racism, no more sexism, no more executions, no more abortions, no more greed, no more environmental destruction, no more killing, no more violence.

Death will not get the last word. Every tear will be wiped away, and we will learn to embrace one another as sisters and brothers.

All we have to do is open our eyes, join hands with one another, and take another step forward on the road to peace.

Acknowledgments

The author and publisher gratefully acknowledge permission to reprint material from the following sources:

Excerpt from "Dom Helder Camara at the Nuclear Test Site" by Denise Levertov, in *Sands of the Well*. Copyright © 1994, 1995, 1996 by Denise Levertov. Reprinted with permission of New Directions Publishing Corp.

Excerpt from "Jerusalem" by Steve Earle. Copyright © 2002 by Steve Earle and Sarangel Music. Reprinted with permission of Wixen Music Publishing, Inc.

Excerpt from "Making Peace" by Denise Levertov, in *Breathing the Water*. Copyright © 1987 by Denise Levertov. Reprinted with permission of New Directions Publishing Corp.

Excerpt from "Protesters" by Denise Levertov, in *Evening Train*. Copyright © 1992 by Denise Levertov. Reprinted with permission of New Directions Publishing Corp.

"The Letter" by Sherrill Hogen. Reprinted with the author's permission.

"The Wisdom of Thomas Merton" by John Dear, published in a slightly different version in *The Merton Annual*, no. 19, ed. Victor Kramer. Louisville, Ky.: Fons Vitae, 2007. Reprinted with permission.

Various articles from the *National Catholic Reporter* (www.ncrcafe.org) by John Dear. Reprinted with permission.

About the Author

John Dear is an internationally known voice for peace and Christian non-violence. A priest, pastor, and peacemaker, he has served as director of the Fellowship of Reconciliation, the largest interfaith peace organization in the United States. After September 11, he was a Red Cross coordinator of chaplains at the Family Assistance Center in New York, and he counseled thousands of relatives and rescue workers. He has traveled the war zones of the world, been arrested some seventy-five times for peace, led Nobel Peace Prize winners to Iraq, and given thousands of lectures on peace across the United States and the world. He lives in the desert of northern New Mexico.

He writes a weekly column for the *National Catholic Reporter* and has written numerous books, including *Transfiguration; You Will Be My Witnesses; Living Peace; The Questions of Jesus; The God of Peace; Jesus the Rebel; Peace behind Bars; Mary of Nazareth, Prophet of Peace; The Sound of Listening; Mohandas Gandhi;* and *Disarming the Heart*. He is also the subject of a documentary film called *The Narrow Path*. He has recently been nominated for the Nobel Peace Prize. (For more information, see www.johndear.org.)